FORT Wellington

The British in North Australia 1827–29

Derek Pugh OAM

Forewords by The Hon. Austin Asche AC QC
and Dr Brian Reid

Derek Pugh OAM: Author
Fort Wellington: The British in North Australia 1827–29
Text ©Derek Pugh 2020
Original Photographs ©Derek Pugh 2020

ISBN: 978-0-6481421-1-9

Design and layout by Michael Pugh: michael.pugh@bigpond.com

Notes: Includes bibliographical references and index.
Subjects:
Northern Territory—History, British settlement attempts
Aborigines:—Iwaidja—Early contact—History Aboriginal-European relations
3rd Regiment of Foot—Royal Marines
Convicts—Crown Prisoners
Pioneers: Northern Territory—social conditions—health—scurvy
Macassan Trepang industry
Diarists: Collet Barker—Dr Braidwood Wilson—Dr Duncan
Commandants Captain Collet Barker—Captain Henry Smyth—Lieutenant George Sleeman
Fort Wellington—Cobourg Peninsula—Port Essington
Buffaloes and pigs—introduction to Australia
Shipwrecks—Torres Strait

Also, by Derek Pugh:
Darwin: Origin of a City.
Darwin 1869: The Second Northern Territory Expedition.
Escape Cliffs: The First Northern Territory Expedition 1864–66.
Fort Dundas: The British in North Australia: 1824–29.
Turn Left at the Devil Tree.
Tambora: Travels in Sumbawa and the Mountain that Changed the World.
Tammy Damulkurra (2nd edition).
Schoolies.
The Owner's Guide to the Teenage Brain (2nd edition).

Front Cover: Phillip Parker King, 1818, Raffles Bay, SLNSW FL1032654.

Contact:
derekpugh1@gmail.com,
www.derekpugh.com.au

NATIONAL LIBRARY OF AUSTRALIA

A catalogue record for this book is available from the National Library of Australia

Acknowledgements

I am indebted to a number of people in the preparation of this book. In particular are two Territorians of note, both recorders and creators of NT history in their own right. When I met The Honourable Austin Asche, AC QC, I quickly asked him if he'd like to read and comment on the manuscript, and even write a foreword for me. He agreed immediately. I explained to him that I thought he was the right person to write about the Territory's history, because, at 94 years, he's lived more than half of it (at least, since settlement), led it as the Administrator, in the courts, and as a member of Norforce. Few have as much knowledge about the Territory as does His Honour.

Dr Brian Reid is another Territory treasure. For many years, he has been a stalwart of the Historical Society, an eminent history scholar and a participant in research expeditions to Fort Wellington (and other places of note), and an author of a number of history books. He also kindly accepted my invitation to read the manuscript and write a foreword. My thanks go to both these gentlemen for their contribution and support. Who says you can't have two forewords in a book ...?

My friend and neighbour, Peter Whelan was once again an early reader and hunter of miscreant commas. It takes a village to edit a book and help from friendly readers is essential. Thanks too, to Michael Pugh for editing and design of the finished tome—he's really good at it. And to Dr Murray Garde, who has regularly received my anthropologically orientated questions with good grace and erudition, and I have neglected to thank in previous books.

This project has been supported by the Northern Territory Government through the Northern Territory History Grants Program of the Department of Tourism, Sport and Culture. These grants are essential to history writers like me—without them, unique stories, like the events that occurred at Fort Wellington, would remain hidden in dusty old archives (I know that's not fair—the archives are kept meticulously, and besides, many of them are now stored electronically). So, of course, my thanks go to the staff of the Northern Territory Archives and Library Service (again), the Australian National Library, especially those who have digitised thousands of newspapers, and other resources from Australia's past, on www.trove.nla.gov.au, and Anthony Duffield at SLSA. They are the rocks upon which much of my research depends.

Derek Pugh

Contents

Table of illustrations

Table of maps

Foreword
The Honourable Austin Asche, AC QC

The old adage that the British acquired their overseas possessions 'in a fit of absence of mind', seems to be the only explanation why, having planted the Flag at Botany Bay, they thereby acquired vast areas of New Holland, although they had no more than casually explored very small areas of it.

Phillip Parker King, in 1820, mapped out the northernmost boundaries of that part of the continent that later became Queensland and the Northern Territory, and the first signal to all nations that this was now, and would forever remain, within the sovereignty of Great Britain was a settlement at Fort Dundas, (Melville Island), in 1824. This was followed by two further settlements at Fort Wellington (Raffles Bay) in 1827, and Port Essington in 1838.

The assumption of sovereignty was prompted, in part, from some concern over potential claims by the French and, in part, by possible commercial contacts leading to trade with Asia.

It is doubtful that the French were serious. They had, after all, sold the whole of Louisiana to the USA in 1803, which hardly constitutes a passionate enthusiasm to plant colonies. They were also diverted, within the requisite periods, by the popular French sport of revolution; which they achieved, with great success in 1789, 1830 and 1848; leading up to the splendid achievement of 1870. They were never really serious about Australia. Their colonial ambitions lay closer to Africa.*

So far as trade with Asia was concerned, the settlements were not particularly well placed for this purpose, and Singapore was already emerging as the success that it became.

All three settlements failed. There is really no more polite word for it, though in the case of Fort Wellington it was a dereliction of an overseas bureaucracy, rather than the settlers themselves.

It is the history of this settlement that Derek Pugh traces in fascinating detail. Those who travelled to Fort Wellington were a true cross-section of that strange mixture of humanity that was slowly and painfully developing from a convict past to a gradually more prosperous and hopeful future. There were the clearly categorised classes of leaders, free settlers, soldiers, marines, cooks, servants and convicts. Within this motley group Derek has found personalities, sad and inspiring, failures and successes, those who met challenges splendidly, and those who suffered miserably. The ultimate lesson is that nothing has changed. The same combination of personalities can be found today. Apart from material circumstances, has anything changed in human nature?

It is helpful to have been given the full text of contemporary letters rather than extracts, so that one gets a more exact picture of the times. This is enhanced by the series of letters set out in full in Appendix B of the book.

The special challenge to this basically European community was the encounter with the very different long-settled culture of the original inhabitants. The same problems were being met throughout the continent with very similar results. There were enlightened characters such as Captain Barker who offered friendship and, generally, received it; there were others who felt threatened by constant thefts of equipment, and were prepared to retaliate. Equally, on the other side, there were hostile and friendly elements. Basic misunderstandings prevailed here as everywhere.

---

* This paragraph need not be read by professional historians.

In the end, three expeditions (Fort Dundas, Fort Wellington and Port Essington) were failures, or, at least, were not permitted to succeed. Between 1824 and 1849 the British Government, having cast the three ventures into the water, allowed them to sink without trace of Imperial Concern. No further attempts to settle took place until 1864, and then it was the Colony of South Australia (which had, by then, swallowed the Northern Territory) who did the settling. The result was Escape Cliffs (disaster) in 1864 and Palmerston (Darwin) in 1869 (success). And so, the story continues ...

It is relevant to observe that, throughout his careful description of the events, from the founding to the abandonment of Fort Wellington, Derek retains an objective view. So, we don't have lectures on our improvement or deterioration (it depends on what you feel) from the past, or the 'lessons' to be learnt. The reader can enjoy a true narrative, well told, and without the sermon.

Austin Asche
Patron, Historical Society of the Northern Territory

Foreword
Dr Brian Reid

Fort Wellington, Raffles Bay, on the Northern Territory's Cobourg Peninsula, was the second of the three military establishments erected by Britain's Colonial Office in North Australia in the first half of the nineteenth century. It endured for the shortest time of the three settlements but, ironically, had the best prospect of surviving had it not been prematurely abandoned. It is about this settlement that Derek Pugh has put together an absorbing and detailed narrative.

The story begins with a broad overview of settlement attempts in North Australia, particularly the earlier establishment of Fort Dundas on Melville Island, before embarking on a chronological account of Fort Wellington. We are fortunate in having, as sources for this settlement in addition to the official documents, diaries by settlement members, especially Collet Barker and Braidwood Wilson, and the meticulously assembled biographies of the settlement convicts by Edward Street. Derek Pugh has used all these sources to wonderfully detail the daily life of the settlement; the people who came, went and stayed and the ships that protected, provided for and visited the little settlement.

Commandant Collet Barker stands tall in the history of this settlement and the narrative pursues his life, career and effectiveness as officer in charge closely. He demonstrated, unusually for his time, that it was possible to relate respectfully to the Iwaidja, the local Aboriginal people. The narrative also details Barker's tragic death on a sand dune in South Australia.

Derek Pugh has spent many years teaching in Aboriginal communities in the Top End and the understandings he retains from this experience has enabled him to bring to life the original people of the Cobourg Peninsula, the Iwaidja. They are an important part of the narrative, not just a background, especially during the time of Collet Barker.

This work is a useful addition to the growing history of North Australian Colonial settlements. It is also a wonderful description of the daily life of Fort Wellington and should be read by all with an interest in that aspect of our history.

Dr Brian Reid
Historical Society of the Northern Territory

Timeline
Fort Wellington

'Since the beginning'	The land is owned by the Iwaidja and their forebears since the Dreamtime.
About 1780	Macassan trepang fishermen start making annual visits to collect trepang.
1803	Matthew Flinders passes by on the *Investigator*.
1820	P.P. King, in the *Mermaid*, maps and names Raffles Bay after Sir Stamford Raffles.
26 September 1824	Possession formally taken of Melville Island by Captain Bremer and the NSW border is moved west to the 39th parallel.
21 October 1824	Fort Dundas formally established and named (anniversary of the Battle of Trafalgar).
17 April 1826	Earl Bathurst orders Governor Darling to investigate starting a second settlement on the north coast, east of Fort Dundas.
19 May 1827	*HMS Success* and *Marquis of Lansdown* depart Port Jackson for 'Port Essington' with 30 soldiers of the 39th Regiment of Foot, 12 Royal Marines and 22 Crown Prisoners, two women, 5 children.
May 1827	*HMS Mary Elizabeth*, under Lt Hicks, drops behind *Success* and *Marquis of Lansdown* and arrives a few weeks after. She goes first to Fort Dundas.
15 June 1827	*HMS Success* arrives at Croker Island but Captain Stirling discounts it as a site for settlement. He sends men to evaluate Raffles Bay.

18 June 1827	Fort Wellington is established on the eastern shore of Raffles Bay (anniversary of the Battle of Waterloo).
26 June 1827	Iwaidja men steal a whaleboat and remove all iron from it.
11 July 1827	Two Iwaidja men, Mariac and Iacama, meet Commandant Smyth. He nicknames them 'Wellington' and 'Waterloo'.
18 July 1827	The brig *Mary Elizabeth* finally arrives in Raffles Bay, a month after Fort Wellington was established.
25 July 1827	Captain Stirling and the *Success* sail away, leaving Captain Smyth in charge.
28 July 1827	Private James Taylor speared non-fatally in the back. The spear entered a lung.
30 July 1827	Captain Smyth orders an 18-pound cannon to be fired at the Iwaidja near the fort and orders the soldiers to catch someone. One Iwaidja killed by rifle fire, others wounded. None were captured.
August 1827	Scurvy and/or fever starts to appear among the settlers.
15 October 1827	Dr Cornelius Wood dies of fever, after previously trying to commit suicide.
October 1827	Major Campbell and John Radford, from Fort Dundas, visit. They return to Melville Island and take the 13 sickest men to the Fort Dundas hospital (including Pte James Taylor), unaware that Dr Gold had been murdered outside Fort Dundas in their absence. They eventually are sent to Sydney.
28 December 1827	Smyth orders a hunting party to capture an Iwaidja person. A camp was attacked at night: one man killed ('dispatched' out of his misery); one woman bayonetted and killed; one small child drowned; one small girl (named Reveral), injured and captured. The men earned a £5 reward.
28 March 1828	Several Macassan praus arrive and are invited to visit the fort.

17 April 1878	Lt George Sleeman arrives on the *Governor Phillip* and replaces Captain Smyth. Dr Robert Davis, Assistant Surgeon, replaces the deceased Dr Wood. Also, on board were Captain Hartley and Dr Sherwin, heading to Fort Dundas. Captain Smyth and Major Campbell later return to Sydney together on the *Governor Phillip*.
13 September 1828	Collet Barker arrives to take over from Lt Sleeman when the *Governor Phillip* returns. Lt Sleeman is transferred to be commandant of the new penal settlement at King George's Sound.(Albany WA)
September 1828	*HMS Satellite* under Captain Laws visits both Fort Wellington and Fort Dundas. Captain Laws writes a positive report about the settlements (see Appendix 2).
3 October 1828	Private John Cook disappears in the bush. He is never seen again. Mrs Cook is left behind, and Barker allows her to stay at the fort until it is abandoned.
17 October 1828	Four Crown Prisoners escape in a whale boat. They are never seen again.
November 1828	In London, the decision is made to abandon Fort Wellington.
25 November 1828	The British have their first meeting with Iwaidja men since December 1828.
2 December 1929	Barker meets some Iwaidja men, including 'Wellington'.
7 December 1829	'Wellington' and 'Waterloo' visit the settlement for the first time after being led in by hand by Nonie, daughter of Oodeen.
26 December 1829	Relationships with the Iwaidja so improved that three men stay overnight in the settlement, in a tent, for the first time.
January 1829	In London, the decision is made to establish a new settlement at Swan River in W.A., with Captain Stirling in charge.

14 February 1829	*HMS Amity* and *HMS Lucy Ann* arrive with stores and orders for Fort Dundas, Melville Island to be abandoned. 13 Crown Prisoners transferred from Fort Dundas, including Mary Rycroft and seven soldiers of the 57th regiment also transfer.
April 1829	A large number of praus begin to arrive from Macassar.
10 May 1829	*HMS Amity,* under Captain Owen, is sent to Timor for buffaloes, sheep, fresh food, etc. On board is John Radford.
13 June 1829	*HMS Mermaid* wrecked in Torres Strait, her crew transferred to *Swiftsure,* until she too was wrecked off Cape Sidmouth on 5 July.
30 June 1829	*HMS Amity* arrives back from Timor with buffaloes and pigs, and Dr Thomas Braidwood Wilson.
25 July 1829	John Radford, the 'Deputy Assistant Commissar General' at both Fort Dundas and Fort Wellington, dies of fever.
28 July 1829	Three ships arrive in Raffles Bay. The *Amity* returns, the frigate *HMS Satellite*, under Captain Laws, and the *Reliance* under Captain Hays.
29 July 1829	Captain Nolbrow (of the *Mermaid*), twice wrecked en-route, arrives on *HMS Resource* with Governor Darling's orders to abandon the settlement. Stores and equipment are to be transferred to the Swan River and the Crown Prisoners to King George's Sound (Albany).
24 August 1829	The chartered merchant ship *Thompson* is loaded in preparation for departure. Several Crown Prisoners are locked on board to avoid their escape. Several others escape but most come back. Two disappear forever.
31 August 1829	Fort Wellington is abandoned.
Dec 1829–March 1831	Captain Barker administers King George's Sound. Later, he is killed at the mouth of the Murray River whilst en-route to New Zealand to be its first Government Resident.
1835	Braidwood Wilson publishes his narrative about Fort Wellington and his travels.

Sept 1838	Victoria Settlement established in Port Essington by Capt Bremer. It lasts for 11 years under Captain John McArthur.
1839	*Astrolabe*, under Captain Dumont d'Urville, visits the site and reports everything overgrown, and the graves tampered with (nails removed).
1870s	A buffalo camp is built on the Fort Wellington site by Dewar, Munro Leslie and Marshall. Water cisterns and chimney remnants are still visible.
1916	A Methodist mission is established on nearby Croker Island.
1924	Cobourg Peninsula is gazetted as a Native Flora and Fauna Reserve.
1931	Arnhem Land declared an Aboriginal reserve.
1966	Historical Society of the Northern Territory: first expedition.
1976	Fort Wellington area proclaimed an historic reserve.
1981	Cobourg Peninsula is the first land granted back to its Aboriginal traditional owners by the Northern Territory Government.
1980–90s	Pearls are farmed in the waters of Raffles Bay.
2009	Historical Society of the Northern Territory run a second expedition. They establish where the fort was situated.
2010	Fort Wellington is registered on the Northern Territory Government Heritage Register.

Preface

In 1824, the British Government planned to establish *two* garrison outposts on the north coast of New Holland that would ensure British ownership of the continent and provide an access point for trade and communications with the East Indies. However, the expedition sent out in mid-1824, under the command of Captain John James Gordon Bremer, had only enough resources to start a single settlement. Bremer took his three ships to Port Essington, a huge navigable waterway that is several times bigger than Sydney Harbour, on the western edge of Arnhem Land. The port had recently been mapped by Phillip Parker King in the *Mermaid*, several years earlier, in 1818, and it was ideally suited to shipping. Macassan trepang fishermen were already known to visit there every year.

Unfortunately, when Bremer's men had a quick look around, they failed to find a source of fresh water large enough to sustain a community the size of which, in Bremer's mind, would rival the quickly burgeoning Singapore. After just a few days, during which four men drowned in a boating accident, Bremer took his little fleet onwards to Melville Island. There, he personally found a spring fed billabong, by falling into it, whilst duck hunting. It was fed by a perennial creek he called Johns Creek.

On a point of land now known as Punata, a kilometre across the bay from the present community of Pirlangimpi, he established Fort Dundas on 21 September 1824. Then, after just a few weeks, Bremer and the *Tamar* sailed away, leaving the new fort under the command of Captain Maurice Barlow, and a detachment of the 3rd Regiment of Foot, known as 'The Buffs'.

The settlers arrived with optimism, hoping to be the pioneers of something big, like Singapore. The city inspired by Sir Stamford Raffles was just five years old and was growing fast, showing huge promise as a trade and strategic possession. Could Fort Dundas do the same? Unfortunately, no.

Pirates took the Fort's two victualling ships in the islands to the north and beheaded their crews, and months went by as supplies dwindled. When no one ever visited, Captain Barlow quickly realised the fort was poorly positioned. In fact, the Macassans, who had fished for *béche-de-mer*, or trepang along the north coast for decades, *never* visited that part of the coast at all, for two reasons: trepang were hard to find there, and, as the British also discovered, the local Tiwi were violent and unwelcoming.

Frightened for decades that the Malays would return as slavers, the Tiwi had closed their island to foreigners, and Barlow and his men were harassed by them in an active resistance to their presence. Men in their huts could suddenly be surprised by a spear thrown through their windows. A Tiwi man was killed by Corporal Gwillan of the Royal Marines, and he was murdered in response. The new settlement, clinging to a tropical island far from shipping lanes or any other civilised settlement, was soon described as a 'hell on Earth' by Lieutenant Everard, the second in command.

It got worse: scurvy and malaria carried off a number of Crown Prisoners and soldiers, and Barlow pleaded to be relieved.

Meanwhile, in the green leather chairs and wood panelled offices of the Admiralty in England, the push for a second settlement was gathering momentum. By April 1826, the Earl of Bathurst read Barlow's negative reports and concluded the settlement on Melville Island was unsatisfactory, but he was as yet unwilling to give up on the plan. Rather, it was better to try again. So, on 7 April, 1826, he instructed Governor Darling to investigate and establish a second settlement on the north coast, east of Melville Island and closer to the trepang fishing grounds (Bathurst, 1826).

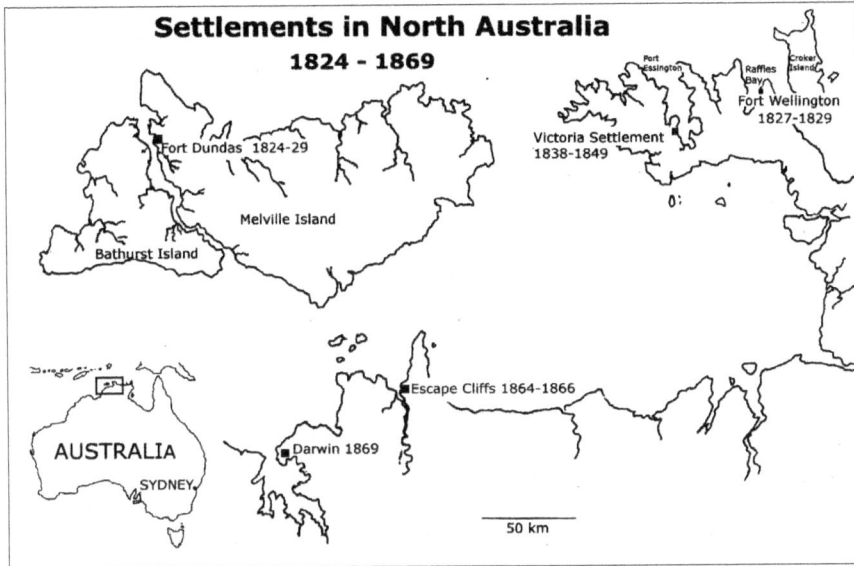

Map 1: Early Northern Territory settlements.

In the meantime, Barlow and the Buffs were replaced by Major John Campbell and the 57th Regiment, 'The Die-Hards', in September 1826. Campbell fared no better than Barlow. Men kept dying and were buried outside the fort.

In Sydney, the Governor formed a plan. A second expedition would travel north and establish a fort in a more appropriate location and, from there, access or create a trade-route with the Macassan trepang fleet. The supplies and equipment could then be transferred from Melville Island, and Fort Dundas abandoned.

For this, another naval officer, Captain James Stirling, was recruited. Unfortunately, for the settlers he would leave behind, his site for a settlement was also hastily chosen. Stirling wasn't interested in exploring the coast to find the best place for a settlement and, within a month of turning the first sod, he was gone. He was in a hurry: he already had his eyes on the greater prize of the Swan River.

Chapter 1

Captain James Stirling

Twelve-year-old James Stirling bade his 14 brothers and sisters goodbye, joined the Royal Navy and headed off to war. The nineteenth century was still young, and the new midshipman appears to have revelled in the action he saw against Napoleon's navy, and he rapidly rose through the ranks to his first command at the age of 21. He demonstrated to the world that he was a remarkable man when he took his sloop, the 28-gun *HMS Brazen*, to the War of 1812 against the United States and brought two captured ships back as valuable prizes (Statham-Drew, 2003).

Figure 1: Captain James Stirling, R.N.

The colonies in Australia were still young. Stirling's second command took him to Tasmania and New South Wales in *HMS Success*, departing London in June 1826. *HMS Success* carried coinage and supplies for the colonies of New South Wales and Tasmania, for that was all there was, except for the military garrison on a distant island in the far north, known as Fort Dundas.

Fort Dundas was failing. Established with high hopes of being another Singapore, no one ever came to trade, and at least 33 Crown Prisoners, soldiers, and settlers would be buried behind the settlement, by the time it was abandoned. However, Earl Henry Bathurst, the Secretary of State for War and the Colonies, was not ready to forsake the coast, and Stirling was appointed to establish a second settlement, east of Fort Dundas. Port Essington would be best, he was told, but Croker Island would do, if it was suitable. He was ordered to pick up troops, convicts and supplies in Sydney, as soon as possible.

The *Success* travelled via South Africa as Major Campbell and the 57th were settling into their island 'hell' on Melville Island. They rounded Cape Leeuwin, on the corner of Western Australia, in early November 1826, for the final stretch east along the south coast. The French explorer Captain Nicholas Baudin had been there 25 years earlier and had explored the *Riviere des Cygnes* or Swan River. He had written eloquently of its beauty and future possibilities, and Stirling itched, even then, to sail a little northward to see the river for himself. But, with the good winds of the 'roaring forties' behind them, the *Success* pressed onwards to Sydney.

A few days after he arrived there, so too did Captain Dumont d'Urville in the *Astrolabe*. Captain d'Urville had already had a good look around, calling at both King George's Sound (Albany WA) and Western Port (near Melbourne). The French were only interested, so they said, in making 'scientific observations'. So too, was the crew of the *Coquille*, under Captain Duperry, who were preparing for another 'scientific' voyage to south west New Holland. The Admiralty worried, and Earl Bathurst was deeply concerned, so Stirling was given covert orders to watch and report on the activities of foreigners during his expedition. It was increasingly important to the British that the whole of New Holland remain in their hands, and the possibility of sharing the continent with the French was horrifying. After all, hadn't many of them already spent half their careers, like Stirling, fighting the French in war?

As luck would have it, despite the protocols of hospitality he was extending to d'Urville, Governor Darling shared these concerns, so Stirling easily persuaded him that there was time, before he was needed to sail north, for a little exploring west. The monsoon season was in full swing in the north and the winds blew the wrong way at that time of year for easy access to Port Essington, so there were several months available whilst they waited for the seasons to change. So, in January and February of 1827, Stirling took the *Success* west and spent three weeks exploring the Swan River and its valley. He was quickly convinced that the Swan River was an excellent site for a colony, and he became its strongest advocate. He even offered to become its first Governor, if only he could get there in time, before the French.

First though, Stirling had his orders and needed to complete the mission of founding a new settlement in the north, and the season was now right. The *Success* and the colonial brigs *Amity*, *Marquis of Lansdown* and *Mary Elizabeth* were readied for departure in Port Jackson. Lieutenant William Hicks commanded the latter, accompanied by his pregnant wife, Sophie and their two-year-old son, also called William. Sophie (ne Hickey) tragically died in childbirth at Fort Dundas on 2 November 1827, and her remains, and those of her unnamed daughter, are buried there.

The ships left Sydney in company on 19 May 1827, heading for Port Essington. Soon the *Mary Elizabeth* fell behind. She carried supplies, soldiers, and convict volunteers for Stirling's new settlement, but few maps of the coast where Stirling eventually dropped anchor, existed, and there was no way of knowing that his little fleet never entered Port Essington at all. As a result, Hicks sailed into an empty port:

> ... *I expected the new Settlement would be formed there, to the great astonishment on my arrival at the said Port, not to find the Ships or any Settlement attempted. I waited a week expecting H.M. Ship and Transport every day; after remaining the above time, I proceeded to Melville Island to get any information I could. I arrived on the 8th July. I found H.M. Col. Brig Amity had acquainted the Commandant of that Settlement, That the new Settlement was formed in Raffles Bay; with the least delay possible I got ready for Sea, and proceeded to Port Raffles, where I had the pleasure of arriving last evening, After a long and hazardous passage and the Brig making 2 feet of Water per hour*

*and otherwise in a bad state, but have the satisfaction to say I
have not a single person sick during our voyage, out of upwards 40
persons on board. (Lt Hicks to Capt Smyth 19 July 1827 (Smyth,
1827a)).*

The new settlement was to be commanded by a soldier, Captain
Henry Smyth, of the 39th Regiment of Foot. The pattern, whereby
the colony was founded by a naval officer before being handed over
to the army, as had happened at Fort Dundas, was again followed.
On board the ships were 30 soldiers of the 39th, 14 Royal Marines,
and 22 convict volunteers. Like the earlier Melville Island settlement,
skilled 'mechanic' convicts had been recruited as volunteers to work
in the fort and they expected to be rewarded with an early 'Ticket
of Leave' after just twelve months service. Over the two years Fort
Wellington existed, around 63 Crown Prisoners spent time in the
fort, including those that were transferred from Fort Dundas and
some later arrivals (see Appendix 1). At least 24 of them were in New
Holland on life sentences, and ten for 14 years. To volunteer a year
at a distant settlement seemed a small price to pay for early Tickets of
Leave, and perhaps freedom.

The *Success* arrived off Croker Island on 15 June, and dropped
anchor in Palm Bay, off the western coast. Stirling took a quick
reconnoitre of the island but found no suitable site where he could
establish a city, so he then sent a boat across to the mainland to
explore Raffles Bay. This bay was named by Phillip Parker King in
1818, because from here he had the opportunity of sending a letter to
Sir Stamford Raffles with the captain of a Malay prau (Wilson, 1835).

*... we steered into the bay, and anchored within a small island at
the entrance, in time to observe the sun's meridional altitude. The
evening was spent in pulling around the bay, the shores of which
are low, and so overrun with mangroves, that landing was in most
parts impracticable; but a small break in them being observed
under a cliff, we put ashore to examine the country. Here we
found two streams of fresh water, one of which ran over the beach
with some force; but they appeared to be only the drainings of the
country, and to be merely of temporary duration. The soil was here*

*very good, but the trees and the underwood were so thick that we
did not venture far from the boat. A native's basket was found,
and the usual signs of their having lately been hereabouts. We also
landed on a projecting point, at the bottom of the bay, to obtain
bearings, and a second time under a remarkable cliffy point on the
west side, from the summit of which another set of bearings were
obtained, which completed the survey of the port; and we named
it Raffles Bay, in complement to Sir Stamford ... (King's journal,
April 16 1818) (King, 1827).*

This naming honour followed a 19th Century tradition of creating immortality. As John Lort Stokes of *HMS Beagle* put it in 1824: 'Monuments may crumble, but a name endures as long as the world' (Hordern, 1989).

When a freshwater lagoon was discovered and favourable reports came back, Stirling looked no further, and went ashore to take possession of the bay and the surrounding territory on 18 June 1827. In a costly error, he made no attempt to visit Port Essington at all.

Fort Wellington was founded by raising the flag and firing a 21-gun salute with the ship's guns. The soldiers returned the salute from the shore with musket fire, there was a speech and three hearty cheers for the king, and the British Empire had a new colony.

The speed of Stirling's selection of a site for the settlement was remarkable, and the three days it took was in stark contrast to the three weeks he had already spent in the Swan River on a similar task, without any resources to follow it up. The Swan River became Stirling's passionate focus and he had little interest in exploring the northern coast. He was aware of several recommendations for Port Essington, a few hours' sail to the west, but he ignored them. Stirling had his men raise the Union Jack, fire a salute and gave his speech, and that was it. The Crown Prisoners were then instructed to unload the supplies and begin clearing land for a settlement.

The fort was named after Arthur Wellesley, the Duke of Wellington, the hero of the Battle of Waterloo, and from 1827, the Commander-in-Chief of the British Army. Contemporary writers also referred to the settlement as *Port Raffles*, but at least one newspaper was confused, calling it *Fort Waterloo* (Monitor, 1827), perhaps unsurprisingly, as the foundation day, 18 June 1827, is also the anniversary of the battle.

Stirling was keen to hand over command of the settlement to Captain Smyth as quickly as he could, and be on his way:

TO CAPTAIN SMYTH. His Majesty's Ship Success,

Sir, Raffles Bay, 19 June 1827, off Fort Wellington.

His Excellency General Darling having acquainted me that he has appointed you to take the command of the Settlement to be formed in this neighbourhood, I have the honor to inform you that, in pursuance of my instructions, I have selected the Eastern side of Raffles Bay, near its entrance, as the spot best calculated to meet the views and wishes of His Majesty's Government in the formation of aa establishment in this Quarter, I have in consequence directed such preparations to be made for the reception of yourself and your garrison as time and circumstances have allowed me, and, having taken possession in His Majesty's name of this Territory, and in token thereof displayed His Majesty's Flag, I have to request you will be pleased to assume the command of this Post as soon as you may be enabled to make the necessary arrangements. I have also to acquaint you that, under the circumstances of the case, I feel the necessity of strengthening your force by an addition of marines from this ship, and that I have directed in consequence a Sergeant, Corporal, and 12 Privates to be landed and placed under your command. As this arrangement is made on my own responsibility, you will be pleased to observe that it is to be considered revocable by the Naval Commander in Chief on this Station.

I have, &c,

JAMES STIRLING, Captain. (Smyth, 1827a)

Smyth worried that the bay was too shallow, as the best anchorages were at least a mile from the shore, but of the Fort's site he simply wrote:

… The spot fixed upon is an inclined place about fifty yards from the sea beach, having a fresh water lagoon a little way to the South west of it, which empties itself into the sea by a small

Figure 2: View of Raffles Bay, by Phillip Parker King, 1818 (SLNSW FL1032654).

channel at some distance farther to the west. The country around is flat and thickly wooded, but not encumbered with brush; the soil sandy and indifferent, as far as I am yet able to judge, except about the edges of the lagoon where the grass is luxuriant and the soil rich ... (Smyth, Dispatch #3, 17 July 1827).

The Fort was constructed 'on a bank of Sand not more than five feet above the level of the Sea at high water at Spring tides'. According to the temporary second commandant, Lieutenant Sleeman, there was a better site where 'the most elevated ground near the settlement [commanded] an extensive and beautiful view of the bay, island and adjacent scenery'. The site, which would have 'been a much better situation for a fort than the present one, which scarcely deserves the name ...' (Sleeman, 1828), eventually had a small cottage on it, used by the commissariat, John Radford, and the doctor.

Stirling had been in a rush. His desire to settle near the Swan River was on his mind and the Raffles Bay site was chosen in haste.

He stayed there for only a few weeks, expressed his satisfaction that it was proceeding well, then left Captain Smyth in charge. The hapless Smyth, searching for positives, was impressed by the fishing in the bay, although he had major concerns about his domestic stock:

> ... *The Bay is extensive and well sheltered from the S.E. and S.W. Monsoons, abounding in fish, amongst which are the Baracuta, Mullet and Pomfret, which will be of the utmost importance to us, as I am sorry to say our stock has suffered a considerable diminution since the 10th. The Cattle were sent ashore yesterday and the bull, which ate little during the voyage except pumpkin, is since dead. One of the heifers also broke from its tether soon after being landed and escaped into the woods. I fear much the others will scarcely survive, till they can be confined within bounds, as they appear to be altogether untameable, suffering no one to approach them even with food or drink; besides this, two pigs, one Sheep, one goat and almost all the Poultry have died ... (Smyth, August 1827)*

Stirling and the *Success* sailed on to Fort Dundas on 25 July, where he stayed for just four days before heading to Madras and Penang.

Fort Dundas should have taught the British many lessons. Its existence had cost many lives. Of the original 30 Royal Marines who were posted there, for example, nine had died, mostly from disease, and two had been invalided off the island early. The Marines, under the command of Lieutenant Charles Cartwright Williamson, an engineer, were ignored by the government and not relieved when the soldiers of the 3rd Regiment of Foot were replaced by the 57th. Most of them, in fact, remained on Melville Island from the first day of settlement in September 1824 to near the last. Their tour of duty was finally complete when Captain Stirling took ten of them on board the *Success* on 29 July 1827, and a few months later, *HMS Rainbow*, under Captain Rous, took the remainder back to England (Brookshaw, 2013). Their most important contribution to the settlement had been managing the construction of the fort and other buildings.

On the *Success*, the marines made a reasonably quick trip straight home, but not so Stirling, much to his displeasure. He had to endure several months in Ceylon, until he managed to return to England due to an illness he is thought by some to have feigned. In March 1828, he was back in London pressing his case for the Swan River Settlement. He eventually achieved his dream of becoming its first governor.

Chapter 2

His Majesty's 39th Regiment

His Majesty's 39th Regiment of Foot dates from the beginning of the 'War of the Spanish Succession' (1701–14). They saw success when they seized Gibraltar from the Spaniards in 1704, and then defended it against both the Spanish and the French throughout the 1700s. The Regiment also fought in Europe during the Seven Years War (1756–63) and it was the first regiment to serve in India. In 1811, in southern Europe, the soldiers took part in the horrific battle of Albuera, against Napoleon's army, losing 4,000 men out of the second battalion of 10,000 (the French lost 7,000 of their 24,000 men). The 39th then spent time in North America before returning to France for the last part of the Napoleonic Wars, arriving too late for the Battle of Waterloo, but in time to serve in the occupation forces, which they did until 1818, when they were transferred to Ireland.

Figure 3: Soldier of the 39th Regiment.

Between 1825 and 1827, about 900 men of the 39th Regiment were sent to New South Wales, in detachments on 18 separate ships, serving as guards for Crown Prisoners (see jenwilletts.com).

On the *Regalia,* under Captain Burt, the officers in charge of the Crown Prisoners were Surgeon Superintendent James Rutherford and Lieutenant William Sacheverell Coke[*]. Coke was paid £95 for the role and, as a meticulous record keeper and letter writer, his travel out to Australia with Crown Prisoners makes for interesting reading:

> *… I have had a great deal of trouble with two of the prisoners. One of them threatened to throw the mate over board and has sworn to be the death of him before the voyage is over. The other was mutinous but have got rid of him. An escort arrived last night at 11 to take him prisoner to Chatham … The first man I am obliged to keep on board. I got hurt in assisting to seize and bind them down and so did several of the men. The prisoners laughed when loaded pistols were put to their skulls and swore in Irish dreadfully and struck down everyone they could. One of them is suspected of having been concerned in the murder of Major Goring in Ireland … (Hunter, 2015)*

And:

> *… I was on board the convict hulk today. We have to take a terrible bad set with us. They have set the ship (hulk) on fire 5 times during the last fortnight. The guard was obliged to shoot one of them … (Hunter, 2015)*

Things must have settled down, as the *Regalia* only lost one convict to illness during the journey, and she arrived in Port Jackson on 5 August 1826 with 129 Irish convicts, including 20 lifers, there for the term of their natural lives. The Regiment settled into Sydney and Lieutenant Coke seemed to have relished his new role, wondering whether or not he should purchase his commission to the rank of captain, which then cost £1,500.

---

[*]   Lieut. Coke is in this story because he knew Commandant Captain Smyth, who travelled under similar circumstances to NSW. So too did Dr Wilson, and an account of the journey out can be found in his book, *A Narrative of a Voyage Around the World*, from 1836.

As more of the Regiment arrived in sections, it was spread out across the colony. Several of the 39th are remembered in the forefront of Australian history: Explorer Captain Charles Sturt arrived with his detachment in 1827 on the *Mariner*. In 1828, Sturt set out on his first great journey, travelling 1,900 kilometres to the Darling River, which he named after the Governor, and in 1829, he took a party of soldiers and convicts by whaleboat down the Murrumbidgee and the Murray Rivers. Sturt failed to reach the mouth of the Murray during his exploration.

Other famous members were Captain Forbes, also an explorer, and 'Trooper' Michael Muggleston, who shot and killed the 'Wild Colonial Boy', Jack Donahue, a bushranger.

Three officers of the 39th were to command Fort Wellington: Captains Henry Smyth and Collet Barker, and Lieutenant George Sleeman.

Chapter 3
Captain Henry Smyth

Henry Smyth was promoted to Captain, in Ireland on 17 April 1823, and was thus an experienced officer when the Regiment was shipped out to New Holland between 1825 and 1827. It is unclear when he arrived because there was no *Smyth* on any ships' manifest of the time. It is likely he was recorded as Captain *Smith*[*] instead. Smith arrived in Hobart on the *Earl St Vincent* on 13 Aug 1826, and if indeed it was really Henry Smyth, records show that he was married, but his wife died on the journey out. On board with him were Sergeant George Millwood, Corporals Shaw and McDonough, 27 privates, 4 women, 6 children and a cargo of 164 convicts, including 73 lifers.

Henry Smyth had no choice, other than to follow orders when he was sent to Raffles Bay as commandant of the new settlement, and there appears to be little in the record as to why he was chosen. Stirling seemed to like him, and called him 'a gentleman of great sense, great zeal and experience' (Stirling, 8 June 1828) but, as the historian Allan Powell points out, he demonstrated 'precious little of these qualities at Fort Wellington' (Powell, 2016).

Lieutenant Coke knew Captain Smyth and mentioned his departure north in a letter to his father from Newcastle. He didn't hold out much hope for him:

> ... *Capt Smyth sailed 2 months ago to form a settlement at Port Essington. Very few of his men will return as it is so near the*

---

[*]   There is no reference to a Captain Smyth bringing out a detachment of men of the 39th at all. See (BDA, 2019).

*Line and the Malays are very warlike ... The last Vessel that took
Provisions to Melville Island found the Commandant living on
Bandicoot (a kind of Rat) and mice ... (Coke, in (Hunter, 2015).*

Smyth, like the three commandants at Fort Dundas, was an
uninspiring leader who bemoaned his fate and asked for transfer as
soon as possible. However, in his defence, he did make some progress
in the development of the settlement and was building some good
working relationships with the Macassan trepang fishermen.

After Stirling had given the founding speeches, the convicts
and soldiers transferred from the ships to the shores of Raffles Bay.
They then began felling trees for the timber walls of the stockade and
clearing the bush. In a few short weeks the fort was constructed, and
Smyth was left in charge as the navy sailed away in the *Success*, never
to return.

Captain Smyth was required to report to Governor Darling as
often as possible. He did this through the Colonial Secretary of New
South Wales, Alexander MacLeay* and it is largely in these reports
that the early history of the fort is recorded.

Smyth and most of his men had travelled north as passengers on
the *Marquis of Lansdown*, which followed *HMS Success* as closely as
possible up the coast. The journey was reasonably uneventful, marred
only by the *Marquis* spending several hours stuck on an uncharted
sand bar. Other ships travelling with them were the *Amity* and the
Caledonia, and the *Mary Elizabeth* under Lieutenant Hicks. The latter
fell far behind, and Smyth was soon worried:

*... It is with much regret I have to state that the Mary Elizabeth
has separated from us and has not been seen since' 6 P.M. Sunday,
20th of May (the day subsequent to our leaving Sydney). She was
then about 3 leagues astern and making all sail to come up ...
(Smyth, 10 June 1827).*

The loss of the *Mary Elizabeth* would have been a serious blow
to the establishment of the new fort, but Smyth may have been

---

* An avid insect collector, MacLeay started off the collection in The MacLeay
Museum, at the University of Sydney.

particularly worried because he knew that Captain Stirling had not given Lieutenant Hicks any directions to where their destination actually was. All Hicks was told was 'Port Essington':

> ... *I fear the absence of the Mary Elizabeth will very seriously impede our operations at the intended Settlement, the greater part of the Iron work, all the Nails, Spades, Shovels, Axes, Miners' tools and almost every description of necessary implements being aboard of her. The loss of 21 persons, among whom are so many Mechanics of the description so peculiarly necessary, will I am persuaded be also sensibly felt exclusive of so considerable a diminution in our strength ...* (Smyth, 10 June 1827)

> *Nothing whatever has been heard of the Mary Elizabeth; and, although I am well assured Captain Stirling will render us every assistance in his power during his stay here, I cannot but look forward with much anxiety for the welfare and even the safety of the Establishment when left to itself with our diminished means* (Smyth, 9 July 1827).

> *The Brig Mary Elizabeth has not yet arrived; the want of the implements she has on board has retarded our progress considerably ...* (Smyth, Dispatch #3, 17 July 1827)

Much of the fort was built before the *Mary Elizabeth* arrived with the tools, because Captain Stirling was in a rush to leave on the *Success*, and would take the protection the ship provided. By the end of July, Stirling was confident enough in the settlers' security to go:

> ... *As I am not aware that the continuance of H.M.S. Success at this anchorage is necessary ... I propose on Monday next to proceed to Melville Island ...* (Stirling, 22 July 1827).

Fort Wellington was a hexagon of 2-metre-high log walls. Four or six 18-pounder carronades protected its walls. The soldiers' barracks were placed on its south side, the Crown Prisoners' quarters on the north side, and the Royal Marines on the east. Four small huts were built for the married soldiers, and small cookhouses were semi-attached to the barracks. Inside the fort's walls there was a square 6-metre-high tower from which the sentries could observe the entire camp (and fire upon passing Aborigines, which they did with impunity during Smyth's time).

By the time Stirling departed and Smyth took control, much work had been done. The stockade and several huts had been built and the garden cleared of scrub and planted. Stirling described the fort as he left it:

> ... a Hexagonal Stockade formed of Solid Timber buried four feet in the ground and raised seven feet (2.2 metres) above it being composed of Trees in an upright position having at four angles 18-pound Carronades mounted on platforms to fire over the stockade. In the middles of the enclosed space, whose sides average forty-five feet in length, there is a Cavalier or tower. Twenty feet square and twenty feet high, built of solid log work and impervious to musketry, except in the points built for loopholes. Over the solid part of this building there is raised a home for the Commandant, the under Apartments containing in safety almost all the Stores in the settlement. Around the Fort at proper distances and in Condition to flank and protect the side of the Stockade and to be protected, are four houses or barracks for the troops, Marines and Prisoners, built of strong uprights and all completely thatched. Surrounding the whole camp is a rough paling to prevent any body of Men from rushing in the Sentinels ... (Stirling, 1827)

Smyth wrote that all six carronades were mounted on the fort's corners:

> ... A strong Log House and Battery mounting 6 18 Pounders and enclosed by a Stockade 25 feet distant of perpendicular piles 8 feet above the surface, is nearly completed. Three Huts are made for the 39th, the Marines, and the Crown Prisoners, a fourth for a married man and his family, and the whole surrounded by a temporary three railed fence ...
>
> The Garden with some seeds and plants is promising, in others not so; the Peach Trees have taken root but the buds, which were inserted in Sydney, have altogether failed. The Bananas thrive well, also the Sugar Cane. The period is too short as yet for a fair judgment to be formed of what the nature of the soil may be relative to the variety of things already put in it; the extent of the Garden is necessarily confined within a short space contiguous to the source of the Lagoon, and along its banks close to the Settlement. The whole of the Ground I have as yet seen, with the

*exception of the lowest and of that near the small river about 2
Miles to the NE. of the Settlement, is sterile and composed of a
sort of pudding stone, strongly impregnated with Iron; the River
above alluded to takes its rise in a swampy plain about 3 miles to
the East, and, with a few Basons [sic] in its course, maintains a
very small stream for about 5 Miles emptying itself into the Bay to
the N.E. ... (Smyth, Dispatch #3, 17 July 1827).*

The logs were sourced from the forest up and down the coast.
Many were floated to the settlement and a straight cutting was put
through the reef to get them close to the building sites (Frederickson
& DeLaRue, 2013) and a sawpit was dug near it. This cutting remains
as one of the few obvious reminders of the fort's existence on the site
today.

*... Soldiers were quartered in a large barrack, 54 by 18 feet, with
its own detached cookhouse; married men occupied four small
huts. The convicts were housed in two barracks: one measured 26
by 18 feet and the smaller building, constructed of perpendicular
logs covered with bark, was 18 by 14 feet. These buildings were
watched over by a guard house, 20 by 12 feet. The commandant's
office, the storekeeper's area and quarters for the first overseer
shared a structure 36 by 24 feet. The hospital claimed ample space
for thirteen patients, a surgery and attendant's quarters, within an
area of 26 by 18 feet. The Royal Marines shared another hut with
detached cookhouse. Two huts accommodated the second overseer,
stockman, gardener and the married convict couple (Moxham
and Rycroft). Barker planned to build more substantial buildings
and completed a solid cell block with walls of squared vertical
posts. A storehouse 30 feet long was virtually completed and an
engineer's store under construction when news arrived of the
settlement's demise ... The area was dotted with a few other bark
sheds, serving variously as sawpit, pig sties, cattle shed, and boat
shed. Some wells had been sunk, up to 45 feet in depth. There was
a small output of bricks, but basically this was a shanty town ...
(Mulvaney, 1993).*

Finally, on the evening of 18 July, the *Mary Elizabeth* came into
view:

*... The Mary Elizabeth arrived in harbour at six P.M., all hands
well, and cargo safe. She has been to Melville Island, not knowing*

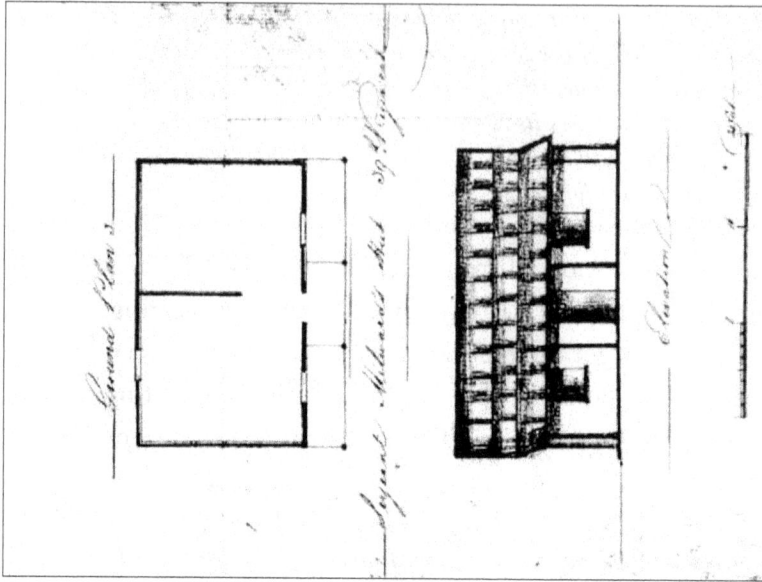

Figure 4:
Plan of the general
store, 1827 NSW
State Archives
NRS906 42059.1.

Figure 5:
Sergeant Milward's
Hut, 1827 (NSW
State Archives
NRS906 42059.1.

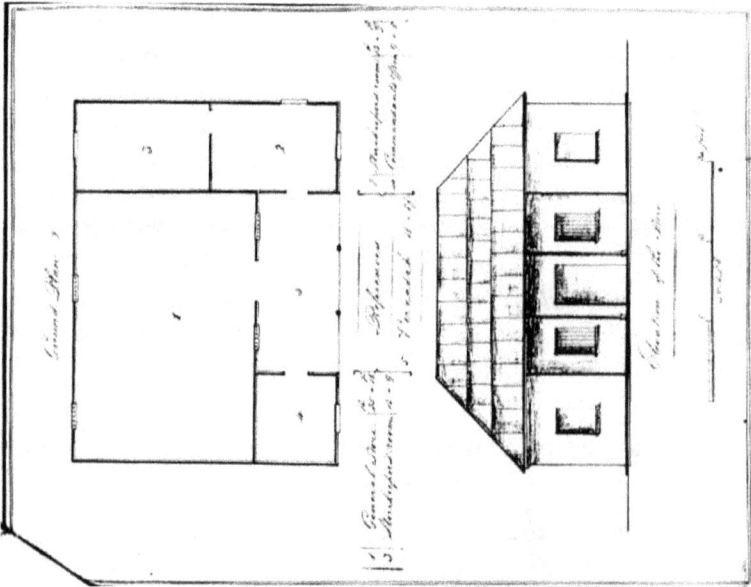

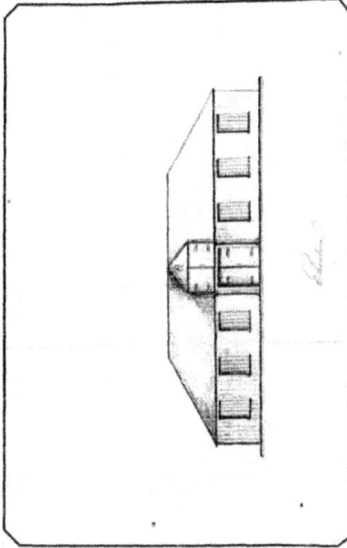

Figure 6:
Hospital, 1827
NSW State Archives
NRS906 42059.1.

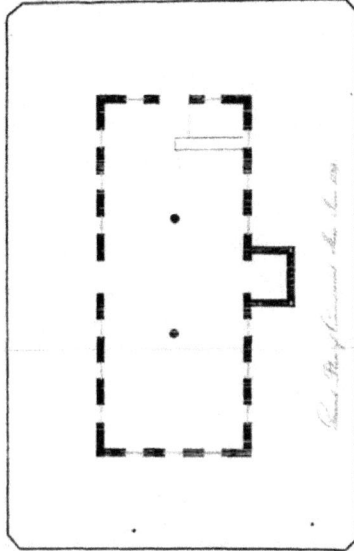

Figure 7:
Commissariat Store,
1829 (NSW State
Archives NRS906
(42060.2).

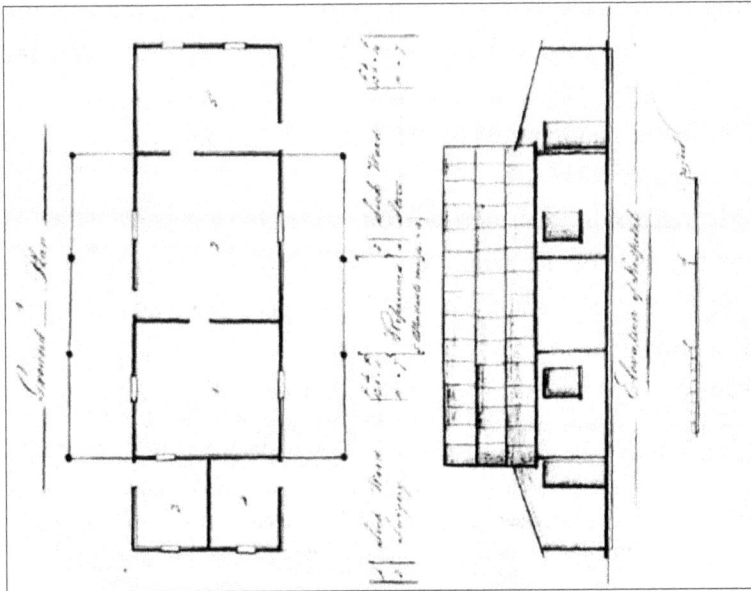

where to find us, and being without a chart of the coast …
(Smyth, 1827 diary).

At last the settlement had a full complement of workers. There were 30 soldiers from the 39th and at least four of their wives and four (or five) children*, 14 Royal Marines off *HMS Success*, Dr Wood the 'assistant surgeon', the commissariat, a 'Malay' interpreter (Oodeen) and 22 Crown Prisoner volunteer tradesmen.

The number of animals brought by the ships was already decimated: the bull died the day it was unloaded after eating nothing but pumpkins for weeks, and several pigs, a sheep, a goat and some poultry had died during the voyage. What was left included several pregnant cows and a young bull, pigs, goats and sheep, and poultry (chickens, ducks and turkeys). The pigs did exceptionally well and several 'farrowed' within a few weeks, thereby increasing the stock enough for Commandant Sleeman to later sell some in an auction (later, many pigs and piglets died from unknown diseases and infection by worms—Barker wrote that 'worms' cascaded from a pig's mouth once it had been hung up). The pregnant cows delivered two fine calves, and buffaloes were soon brought from Melville Island (23 by the brig *Ann* on 20 March 1828) and more, later, from Timor. They were cared for by convict stockmen, though unfortunately, one of those, William Leak (aka 'Leek' and 'Locke'), died on 23 April 1828. 'His death is a great loss to the Settlement as regards the care of the Stock' wrote Smyth.

With Macassan fishermen visiting the north coast annually, an important member of the settlement was the Malay interpreter. His name was Oodeen, but from the first day his name was adapted, and he became known as O'Dean, as if he was of Irish descent. He was an ex-drum-major who had fought on the frontline with the Dutch Ambonese Regiment and the British Malay Regiment. His crime was

---

* George Little, Nonie Oodeen and Coopy (Oodeen?) are the only children to be named in the diaries. George owned a pet monkey. Later Reveral ('Mary Raffles') lived with the Littles. In February 1829, six children and the 'native girl' were listed on the population return.

that he defected to the Kandyan Army*, in 1803, to fight against the British and he was arrested in 1815, tried, and sentenced to death for desertion. His sentence was commuted to transportation to New South Wales for life and he arrived in Sydney, unusually, with his Singhalese wife and their three children.

Oodeen was tall and dark, 'approaching to black' and 'appeared to be intelligent' (*Sydney Gazette* 17 Feb 1816). He initially served as a night watchman in Sydney and quickly became trusted and well respected. He was literate and spoke Malay, Singhalese and Tamil. He was also Islamic, something he had in common with the Macassan trepang fishermen in north Australia. All this brought him to the attention of the authorities, and he was granted a ticket of leave and offered a job as government interpreter at Fort Wellington on a salary of £70 per annum. He was 54 years old, with a growing family, and this seemed a substantial improvement on what he could achieve in Sydney.

Oodeen wasn't called upon to interpret anything for over half a year, and thus had time to build his own house and settle into the fledgling community. In fact, it wasn't until seven months after his arrival that the first Macassan prau was, at last, seen in the distance.

By 1827, Macassan trepang fishermen had been visiting the shores of northern Australia annually for about 50 years (MacKnight, 2017). Trepang, *béche-de-mer,* or 'sea cucumbers' were a valuable delicacy traded by the Macassans to China (MacKnight, 1976). Ironically, fishing for trepang was northern Australia's first international industry, but the peculiar animals, known these days more commonly as 'sea slugs' were eaten by neither the Aborigines of the north, nor the Macassans who came so far to gather them. Instead, according to Ernestine Hill 'trepang soup was the elixir of youth to portly old mandarins, fathers of innumerable sons, and a pick-me-up after the opium pipe' (Hill, 1951).

---

* The Kandyan Wars were fought between the central Sri Lankan Kingdom of Kandy and the British between 1796 and 1815.

In 1803, Matthew Flinders had met the crews of six praus[*] when he was mapping the coastline during his voyage. He had seen signs of some 'foreign people' for many weeks on different islands in the form of stone fire pits, broken pottery and the 'remains of blue cotton trowsers, of the fashion called moormans' [sic] (Flinders, 1803). When he met them, the *Investigator* was then in the English Company Islands off the coast of Arnhem Land, and their leader, or *nakhodka,* was an elderly man named Pobasso. The fleet, Flinders discovered, belonged to the 'Raja of Boni' and fortuitously, he had employed a Malay cook who was able to interpret for him. Pobasso told the Englishman that he had travelled there on at least six previous years out of the past 20 and had been among the first Macassans to do so[†].

Each of the praus weighed about 25 tons and held a crew of 20 to 25 men. They were armed with small Dutch carronades, and the captains and some of the men carried *keris* daggers. Pobasso was surprised to learn of the Port Jackson settlement, as he had never seen foreign ships in the region. He also warned that his men 'sometimes had skirmishes with the native inhabitants of the coast' (Flinders, 1814) and he himself had been speared in his knee.

Twenty-five years later, Deing Riolo was the *nakhodka* of a fleet of 41 praus that had left Macassar in December 1827. It arrived in the waters off Raffles Bay on 20 February 1828. Smyth had erected a flag on the small island at the opening of Raffles Bay to attract attention but it was cut down by the Malays as they mistook it for a 'wrecked ship' sign, and three praus, led by Deing Riolo, entered the bay to investigate. As soon as they were spotted, Captain Smyth sent Oodeen and George Macleod, the storekeeper, with a letter inviting them to call at the settlement, and soon he was welcoming the crews as honoured guests.

---

[*]   These small boats are also known as proas or prahus.

[†]   This dates the first Macassan praus visiting the northern coast to about 1773 although MacKnight concludes that the annual hunt started in these waters in 1780 (MacKnight, 2017). There is evidence that they may have been visiting the Kimberley coast for many years before this.

Both leaders were guided by Oodeen's cultural knowledge and experience. Riolo and Smyth were able to exchange gifts and the two captains got along well. Smyth wrote that Riolo was 'a most polite, graceful Malay [who] made us several presents' (*Sydney Gazette* 11 July 1828) and said he was 'delighted at the prospect of being protected from the natives, who wage war with them' (Wilson, 1835). Smyth hoped their friendship would pay dividends to the British. The Macassans sought and received permission to set up a boiling station* for their trepang on the beach near the fort and Smyth was then able to observe their operation, including the Malays' method of fishing for the sea slugs:

> ... *Sunday, the 30th March ... 10 Boilers were fixed and a number of well-constructed sheds of Bamboo for drying the Beech de Mer and sleeping in ...*
>
> *Monday, 30th March ... At 7 o'clock in the evening, by my permission the Malays about 30 in number commenced fishing along the coast in front of the Settlement; the moon was bright, and I had an opportunity of seeing the very regular manner in which they compassed and examined the whole ground over which they went a distance of about a mile in length and from seven or eight hundred yards from the shore, in any depth of water not above their chins, carrying a spear to bring the slug from the bottom as they are felt with the feet. I restricted their fishing within a given distance of the shore; this novel and unusual sight engaged the attention of the dogs and made them restless the whole night ...*
>
> *Wednesday, 2nd April, The Malays continue to fish with success and are very happy; The Nacodas, Bappa Logo, Deing Riolo, and Bappa Kaseipa, accompanied me through the Garden and were evidently pleased with this mark of my attention; Deing Riolo appeared well acquainted with most of the plants and at my request has promised to bring a variety of the Makassar plants and seeds on his next visit to the Coast.*
>
> *Wednesday, 9th April, Presented each of the Nacodas with 5 yards of printed Calico, 3 yards of white Calico, 1 yard of small*

---

* A line of stones for this boiling station was visible up to at least 2005, but it was destroyed during a cyclone.

*print, and 1 Pocket Handkerchief, as a token of friendship and
remembrance of the British Settlement in Raffles Bay; much
delight and gratitude was evinced for these presents; I subsequently
presented Deing Riolo with a Hand saw, a hammer, 3 Gimblets
and a pair of scissars, and Bappa Logo with some few articles of
a similar kind. Malay characters were painted by the Nephew
of Deing Riolo on a board fixed to the flag staff last erected, for
which I gave him a pair of Scissors ...*

*Friday, 11th April, My Friend, Daeng Riolo, breakfasted with
me, and we had much conversation on the scale of Commerce
with Macassar; he expressed his wish to come and settle in Raffles
Bay with his family, 'being heartily tired of Dutch Oppression'.
In the evening he was taken very unwell but recovered by my
applying Kyapooti oil to his temples. I went on board with him
and personally presented the whole of his crew with a cotton
handkerchief each, and to the Officers (Durumoodies) a pair
of scissors; they were eager to get razors, which I discovered was
for the purpose of making spurs for their game Cocks to fight
with. Daeng Riolo at my entreaty, and I am persuaded with
inconvenience to himself, sold me a Canoe for 5 Dollars; we
parted with numerous mutual good wishes, and, the wind being
favorable, they immediately weighed anchor and sailed; the poor
old man shed tears ... (Smyth, 18th July, 1828).*

On 8 March 1817, the *Fame*, under Captain Henry Dale, arrived at Port Jackson with 198 male prisoners (122 of them on life sentences) from England. On board was Paolo Sois, an Indian 'Lascar'* crewman. After unloading the cargo of prisoners, the *Fame* sailed north to return to England via Batavia and Bengal but, unfortunately, she was wrecked in the Torres Strait. There were survivors, and a few of them, including Paolo Sois, managed to row a leaky boat for two days to reach Flinders Peninsula, on the north coast of Arnhem Land. Ten years later, Lieutenant Hicks, in the *Mary Elizabeth*, picked Sois up, and took him to Raffles Bay:

*... Thursday, July 19th ... Mr. Hicks brought a Portuguese,
belonging to Madras, from Cape Flinders, who had been wrecked[†]*

---

* *Lascars* were sailors or militiamen from India, South East Asia or the Middle East, employed on European ships from 1700 until about 1950.

† Here Smyth gives a different ship's name and another captain: 'in the *Frederic*,

*... about seven years ago; himself, and two others only, escaped in
a small boat, and got ashore, where they both died, leaving himself
the only survivor. We saw the man making a signal, by waving a
branch when we passed two days before the Mary Elizabeth came
there; but mistook him, from his colour, to be one of the natives.
He is anxious to get on to Madras. I have given directions that he
receives rations during his stay with us ... (Smyth, 1827 diary).*

Time had become confused—Sois thought he had survived only
six or seven years. He was a curiosity indeed: his companions had all
died within a year of being shipwrecked, but he had prospered among
the people of the coast and was treated by them kindly. Dr Duncan, on
board the *Mary Elizabeth*, was keen to record Sois' story in his diary. He
heard that his saviours were warlike and constantly in battles with their
neighbours, but they would not let him participate in the fights. Sois
was 'married' and had several children, whom he had abandoned when
rescued by Hicks. His extended time with the northern tribe made him
a valuable recorder of their history and culture:

*... They punish an adulterer, when detected, with death. They
have no knowledge of ships; their chief conversation is either
concerning food or war. There are very few diseases amongst them,
and they in general live to a good old age. They employ themselves
in hunting or fishing during the day, and at night sleep round
a small fire. When a brother dies and leaves a wife, the next
eldest brother marries her. They have no houses or anything to
cover them; and scarcely two tribes speak the same language ...
(Duncan, 1827).*

The Lascar was excited to see the *Mary Elizabeth* come close
enough to signal from the shore, but the locals didn't want him to
leave:

*... The natives were greatly attached to this Lascar. When he
hailed the brig, they placed their hands on his mouth; on the
approach of the boat to carry him on board the brig they fled, but
again returned; but would not go on board the vessel ...*

Unsurprisingly because he had lived in a distant part of the
coast, Sois could not speak Iwaidja, the local language, and was thus

---

Captain Williams, a trader'.

not useful as an interpreter at the new settlement, but he had great knowledge of the bush.

Sois was given work in the gardens, and he was later dropped off in Timor by the *Mary Elizabeth* and was taken to Batavia by Monsieur Becharde. He would have liked to have stayed with Becharde, said Duncan, but the merchant found him to be so 'excessively lazy' he wanted nothing to do with him, and he was put on a ship to his hometown, Madras, where he apparently had a wife and a number of other children, whom he hadn't seen for more than a decade (Duncan, 1827).

Within weeks of arrival at Raffles Bay, men began to fall sick. During August and September 1827, 32 cases of scurvy were admitted to hospital, another 10 fell sick in October, and by the end of the month 49 of the 76 people in the settlement were on the sick list (Darling, 25 Feb 1828). Smyth fell ill too, and his malaise would plague him until he was recalled.

Doctor Cornelius Wood then fell dreadfully ill himself on 25 September, and the pain of his illness became unbearable. On 1 October he tried to kill himself by cutting his own throat, but Privates Thomas Smith and Thomas Williams managed to get the knife away from him before he'd done much damage, and Smyth put him under suicide watch. But Wood was desperate and continued to make attempts on his own life. A wound made 'under his breast' by a set of keys left within his reach worried everyone, and his servant, Private William Baylis, later found a pin driven into his chest as far as it could go. Dr Wood's fever seemed to get worse each day and he succumbed to it on 13 October.

Captain Smyth held an enquiry into his death (Smyth, 1827a) and took statements from all the witnesses of Dr Wood's illness. A bottle was placed into the coffin with the deceased. A message inside it announced that it was signed and sealed on 14th October 1827, by Commandant Smyth, and said the following:

> ... *In the Coffin in which this bottle was placed is interred the body of Cornelius Wood, Staff Assistant Surgeon in His Britannic*

*Majesty's Service, and Medical Officer of this Settlement formed
on the 18th of June 1827. He died from 'Synocha' or 'Simple
continued Fever' and ceased to exist at 9 o'clock P.M. 13th October
1827, the 19th day from the commencement of the attack ...*

Now, with 76 men, women, and children in the settlement,
many of them ill and some of them patients in the 13-bed hospital
without a doctor, Smyth sent a message to Melville Island asking for
Dr Gold to come to Raffles Bay to help:

> *... the awful increase of the Scurvy in the Garrison, induced me
to dispatch the Mary Elizabeth on the 1st of October to Melville
Island, requesting Doctor Gold might be sent to our assistance; on
the 27th Major Campbell and Mr. Radford of the Commissariat
in the Mermaid Ketch arrived here, but I am grieved to say
without the Surgeon and without Lime Juice or any acids to
our assistance except Vinegar, which alone appears by Thomas's
Modern practice of Physic, Page 702, to be of little or no utility;
the small proportion of Nitrate of Potass sent for the Settlement
prevents my trying the Solution of it with common Vinegar (as
stated in the same Page to have proved itself of much Service);
thus I am unhappily situated with only 4 bottles of Lime Juice for
30 requisite cases, and as a preventative I should be most happy
that the whole garrison could have it until at least Vegetables can
be raised ... (Smyth, Dispatch #3, 17 July 1827).*

Major Campbell and the quartermaster, John Radford,
transported the sickest back to Melville Island, but left Smyth to
suffer on:

> *... I have myself some symptoms of it, and there are not more
than 10 men entirely free from it. Major Campbell has been kind
enough to say he will take a few of the worst cases to Melville
Island with him. I have selected 2 cases of Scurvy commencing on
the 6th Augt. and not improved, 1 of Rheumatism of the same
date, and 2 Scurvy cases of a very malignant nature admitted on
the 6th of October, and the Soldier James Taylor, who was speared
by the Natives on the 28th of July ...*

Unfortunately, whilst the *Mary Elizabeth* and her commander,
Lieutenant William Hicks, were away from Fort Dundas, his wife,
Sophie, died in childbirth, and Assistant-Surgeon Gold was murdered

by the Tiwi. A letter from Doctor Gold to his mother described his newfound situation. It is, in hindsight, prophetic:

> ... *this is so unfrequented a part of the world that it is a matter of difficult accomplishment to get away even if I should feel desirous to do so ...the climate is favourable to the production of disease ... The hospital is a small but comfortable building ... and it is generally full. The men have lately suffered from scurvy, malignant fever, and other endemick diseases of a dangerous character. Besides these evils, we are subject to another nearly as formidable. Scarcely a week elapses but our men are endangered by visits of the Aborigines who are very wild and hostile in spite of all the kindness we can possibly show them ... (Bach, 1958).*

Gold is most remembered for his violent death from the very Aborigines he told his mother about. On 2 November 1827, he and John Green, a storekeeper, attended Sophie Hicks' funeral, and afterwards, they went walking towards the gardens outside the settlement, when they met a party of Tiwi. Dr Gold received:

> ... *31 spear wounds, in seven of which the heads were still sticking, several of the spears had gone through the body and head, and one appeared to have penetrated the bowels, several wounds were in his legs, and from every circumstance I should fear he had died very hard ...* (Gazette, 10 March 1825).

There was now no doctor within a thousand kilometres. Campbell tried to find one in Timor, and any medical man could have named his own price to come to the settlement, but no one came forward.

Major Campbell and his men at Fort Dundas were at last replaced by a detachment of the 57th Regiment, under Captain Humphrey Hartley. The newcomers spent a few days in Fort Wellington on their way to Melville Island to take over, and Hartley came away depressed at the poor conditions he had witnessed and the sickness of the people. Under Doctor Sherwin's advice and directions, he brought 13 of the sickest convicts on board *HMS Sir Philip Dundas*, and returned them to Sydney. He reported, two weeks later, to Colonial Secretary MacLeay:

*... The worn out and emaciated condition of the sick at Raffles
Bay and the undue proportion, which their numbers bore to the
numerical strength of the population of that settlement, coupled
with the generally sickly complexion and attenuated appearance of
nearly all afforded a melancholy evidence of the malignant effects
of the climate with which they had been contending and which
with the accumulated local disadvantages Raffles Bay labours
under, appear to render it not only ineligible as a Settlement
but moreover unfit for the presence of civilised man ... (Hartley,
1828).*

Hartley was relieved, and perhaps pleasantly surprised by Fort
Dundas, when he stepped ashore, as only two men were in hospital.
They had plenty of buffaloes and the long dry season lay ahead, so
he felt sure those who were developing scurvy would soon pull out
of it. Hartley was no more aware of the cause of this disease than his
predecessors.

Scurvy is brought on by a deficiency in vitamin C, which
is usually found in fresh vegetables and fruits. It causes a
disintegration of the body's connective tissue, leading to bleeding
gums, loss of teeth, foul-smelling breath, anaemia, lethargy, and
weakness. Long-healed broken bones can separate. It leads to a
slow and painful death if untreated, and more than two million
people died of it during the 'Age of Sail' (Bown, 2003). Throughout
history, scurvy was seen in towns sieged during wars, in prisons, in
countries enduring famines, in remote settlements and in mining
camps. On a poor diet, like the sailors' victuals of salt pork, 'hard
tack' biscuits and grog, it takes only a matter of six weeks for
symptoms to appear.

Lieutenant James Cook is famous for never losing a sailor from
scurvy. Cook ensured his crews ate fruits and vegetables, particularly
limes, which would travel quite well. Surprisingly, even Cook's success
wasn't convincing enough for the medics. Cook's lack of scurvy was
thought to be more to do with 'a want of air sufficiently furnished
with oxygen' (Thomas, 1828).

The First Fleet loaded up with citrus fruit in Rio de Janeiro during its stop there, and no one contracted scurvy after the crew and Crown Prisoners were fed 'great numbers of oranges … (to) put them in a condition to resist the attacks of scurvy' (Collins, 1798). Some understanding then, of the importance of fresh food in the diet, was developing, forty or more years before the northern settlements. It is a wonder that the commandants and medical men of Forts Dundas and Wellington were still so ignorant of the disease.

Dr Turner, the first doctor at Fort Dundas, thought that scurvy resulted from 'privations' arising from 'exhaustion of labour in a tropical environment and exposure to damp during the rainy season' (Turner, 25 May 1825). Turner organised an upgrade of the Crown Prisoners' diet to include preserved meat and spirits in an attempt to fight these privations and avoid scurvy. He was replaced by Dr John Gold, who had no better idea about the causes of scurvy, and men continued to die needlessly, whilst the Tiwi, who had survived on the island for a thousand generations, brimmed with health.

The commandants were military men, untrained in medicine. Major Campbell displayed his ignorance to the Royal Geographical Society in 1834:

> … When the settlement was established in Raffles Bay in 1827, on the north coast of New Holland, and in the same parallel with Fort Dundas, at which place no spirits or wine was issued either to the military or convicts, the scurvy broke out and spread in a rapid and alarming degree, both amongst the soldiers and prisoners … The establishment consisted of young healthy men, direct from Sydney, and many of them only a few months from England. The complaint [scurvy] made its appearance among the settlers in six or seven weeks after landing: their diet consisted of a small quantity of salt meat, and occasionally fish … with flour, sugar, and tea or coffee. When the malady had attacked and rendered incapable of exertion two-thirds of the settlement, spirits, lime juice and sugar made into punch, was issued to all the worst cases, and grog or wine issued to the military. It immediately remitted in virulence, and ultimately nearly or entirely disappeared. I saw all the sufferers myself, having had

*occasion to go to Raffles Bay; and from my observatories and
inquiries, certainly thought that the scurvy there, as well as on
Melville Island was endemic and more dependent on climate and
local causes than diet ... (Campbell, 1834).*

In contrast, however, Campbell thought the Raffles Bay site to
be healthier than the place he had been forced to live:

*... I found the temperature the same as at Fort Dundas; and
on comparing the account of sickness at Raffles Bay with that
on Melville Island, I remarked that they had fewer varieties
of complaints than we had, as also fewer cases of illness in
comparison to their numbers: this I attribute to the air being
less debilitating along the coast of the Cobourg Peninsula ...
(Campbell, 1834).*

Captain Smyth may have been better informed than those at
Melville Island, as he quotes from a newly published text by Robert
Thomas; *Modern Practice of Physic*. He knew that lemon or lime juice
would solve the problem, but did not have enough of it, even for
himself, and he too, suffered symptoms. When Doctor Robert Martin
Davis arrived at the end of April 1828, he naturally immediately
visited the sick and, forewarned by the negative reports he had read,
quickly blamed all the ailments on the climate. His first report to the
government was made in haste, to catch the departing ships, and it
said as much, but over time his observations led to other conclusions:

*... My opinion of this climate has undergone a great change, and
it is now different from what I was induced to form from the
received intelligence of last year. There is no 'endemic' disease here.
The climate of this place surpasses every other as far as I know,
which are equally as near the equator; and were it not for the
great height of atmospheric temperature, I should consider this
climate one of the best in the world ... in (Wilson, 1835).*

In his annual report of 1829, he wrote:

*... This climate has been represented as unfavourable to
European constitutions. I am authorized to declare, after a
residence of fifteen months, that it is by no means so bad as was
imagined. The prevalence of sickness which took place after the
formation of the settlement, can be accounted for as arising from
more satisfactory causes than that of climate. The people were*

unavoidably harassed in clearing ground, felling timber, and building huts, at the same time that the salt provisions, with which they were supplied, proved to be of a very inferior quality, and hardly fit for use: these, with annoyances from the natives, and the gloom and despondency which the death of the surgeon excited, quickly operated in producing scurvy, which was the principal disease amongst the men. A liberal supply of medical comforts, and a superior description of food, have been provided for their use; and, as disease now seldom occurs in any serious form at this settlement, it may be fairly stated, that the climate, instead of being unhealthy, is less so than any other place equally near to the equator.

I was, on my arrival, inclined to consider, that the proximity of the settlement to the Lagoons, with an extensive mud bank in front, (which is occasionally exposed to the influence of the sun,) would tend to make febrile diseases very prevalent, and otherwise operate to the injury of our health; but my conjectures have not been verified. Nothing in the form of epidemic, or contagious disease, has been observed, and the greater proportion of the diseases which have occurred, are to be attributed to the want of a due quantity of vegetable food ... (Davis, 1829).

The causes of scurvy were slowly being unravelled, but whilst they knew of the power of antiscorbutic substances and fresh vegetables, they were too easily sent out without enough of them. Eventually, the masters of ships were required to supply lemon juice and sugar for each person on board as a 'medical comfort'. Dr Wilson, who made several journeys to New Holland in charge of convicts (the largest number was 400 on one ship) wrote:

... lime juice, ... is mixed with water, sugar and wine and issued about a fortnight after we leave England, daily at eleven A.M. and at four P.M. ... (Wilson, 1835).

Wilson noticed that scurvy was more likely to appear on ships after they had passed the Cape of Good Hope if they did not make a port call during the voyage, such as Porto Praya or Rio de Janeiro, where the ship could reload fresh fruit and vegetables. Unfortunately, direct journeys, without stops, began to become normal as sailing technology improved during the nineteenth century. As a result, the ratio of sick convicts crept up. Wilson was aware that the average number of deaths accounted for under two per cent, which, to him, was 'no great mortality', but whilst he clearly saw a link between food and scurvy, even he showed his confusion:

> ... I am inclined to think, however, that if sickness now prevails in an increased ratio, it may be ascribed to the circumstance of the prisoners being embarked soon after their convictions, instead of being, as formerly, for a long time, in the dock-yards, where, their habits being regular, their constitutions became improved ... (Wilson, 1835).

The success of the settlements of the north may have been very different if scurvy hadn't been such an issue. It was not until the gardens started producing enough fresh food that the scourge was kept at bay, but by then it was too late.

Doctor Davis was the first of the English doctors in the north to take any interest in the health of local Aborigines*, albeit from a distance. As the health of his own community improved and fewer patients filled the hospital beds, he had more time to make observations:

> ... It may be justly presumed, that living as they do agreeably to nature, they are subject to fewer diseases than man in a civilised state. However, that they are not altogether exempt from the ills attending animal existence, was very obvious. 'During the inclement and wet weather, at the commencement of this year', observed Dr. Davis, 'a party of the Aborigines was discovered labouring under acute bronchitis, on a low neck of land near the western boundary of Raffles Bay. The symptoms were very severe. During the continuance of the disease they were very abstemious. The only remedies which we saw them employ were (during the severity of the acute stage of the disease) cords tied very tightly

---

* The Aborigines the settlers were meeting belonged to what is now known as the *Iwaidja* tribe. They were consistently referred to as 'natives' by the nineteenth century writers, although Mathew Flinders called them 'Australians'. Alternate names and spellings include *Jiwadja, Juwadja, Iwaija, Eiwaja, Eaewardja, Uwaidja, Unalla.* Once numerous, the tribe was reduced to 30 members by 1881 (7 men, 12 women, 9 boys and 2 girls). Paul Foelsche stated that the community was decimated after Malay traders introduced small pox (known as 'mea-mea' or 'oie-boie') during a visit before 1866 (Foelsche, 1886). Many Iwaidja people today make their home on Croker Island.

round their head, and the frequent pouring of cold water on their heads. On one occasion the chief (Mariac, or Wellington) laid down on the sand, and caused one of his tribe to stand on his head—most probably for the purpose of deadening the acute pain he was suffering ... (Campbell, 1834).

Doctor Davis also suspected that small pox had appeared in the population in previous years:

... Several of these people have deep circular impressions,—on their faces in particular,—as if caused by the small-pox. From the inability of making myself understood, the nature of the disease which produced these marks is not yet ascertained.

The natives described, in language, or, rather, by signs sufficiently significant, the history of this malady, which they call 'oie-boie', and which appears to be very prevalent among them. It evidently bears a resemblance, both in its symptoms and consequences, to small-pox,—being an eruptive disease, attended with fever, and leaving depressions. It frequently destroys the eyes, and I observed more than one native who had thus suffered. Mimaloo's left eye was destroyed by this disease; hence, his English name, One-eye, to which he appeared particularly partial. We could not learn whether they used any remedy, except abstinence. They are also frequently affected with ophthalmia ... (Wilson, 1835).

The Aborigines were first seen by the settlers on Cobourg Peninsula on 22 June. Smyth wrote in his diary:

... Ten or twelve of the natives seen about a mile from camp. They fled on the approach of the watering party from the Lansdown, leaving two spears and a wamero on the ground, which were brought off by the officer in charge of the watering party ... (Smyth, 1827 diary).

No one seemed to be concerned about the officer taking the Aborigines' tools, but quick offence was taken when it was the other way round.

On Sunday 24 June, a group of men were sent to search for a heifer which had strayed. One of them was a little behind the others, and he was 'chased by a number of natives with spears (about seventy or one hundred), who fled on his reaching his party' (Smyth, 1827 diary).

On 26 June, Smyth woke to find that the whaleboat had been taken from its berth during the night:

*... found she had been taken by the natives to the mouth of a
small fresh-water river, about three miles off, hauled up, high
and dry, and stripped of every article of iron about her; both ends
open, and rendered altogether useless ... (Smyth, 1827 diary).*

Dr Duncan, then attached to the *Success*, also kept a diary:

*... On the night of the 26th the natives carried away a whale
boat belonging to Captain Smyth and rendered her completely
useless. She was found next morning near the mouth of a small
rivulet to the northward of the settlement, the greater part of the
iron work being taken out of her, and her planks, &c. broken in
various places, some parts of which were carried some distance
into the bush, several pieces of which I have seen during my
excursions into the woods ... (Duncan, 1827).*

Problems continued. Two iron cooking pots were taken during the night from the cooking fire about 15 metres from where Smyth slept. The sentry challenged the thieves, who dropped the pots in their escape. The next night, 1 July, Aborigines took 150 hammocks which belonged to the *Success*. They were piled on the beach for 'lettering', and were 40 yards from the sentry, who never heard a sound. A ship's officer and 12 marines found some of the hammocks in a search the next day. Over the next week, Smyth's diary relates ongoing visits and increasing contact with the natives:

*... Monday July 2d. ... At twelve, noon, the cooper, with some
other men of the Success, were at the watering place, repairing
the butts, when a party of natives, with spears, came on them; the
retreated, and some of their tools were taken: one spear was thrown,
without injury ... At eleven this night, immediately after the moon
had set, the natives were heard and imperfectly seen, not more than
thirty or forty yards from the sentry: ... he fired at them, as did also
two others of the guard, in the direction they retreated ...
Wednesday July 4th.—The natives, under cover of darkness of the
night, again made their approached about two, a.m., crawling on
their hands and knees. The sentry fired, and I think without effect,
as no cry was heard; they instantly disappeared. ... I had this
day given directions to the guard, that the sentries should remain*

41

totally inactive and quiet, if no more than two or three of the natives made their appearance and allow them to get sufficiently into the settlement to secure them.

Thursday, July 5th.—... Six eighteen-pounder carronades landed from the Success for the fort.

Friday July 6th.—I received a message from Captain Stirling about half-past two this morning, to say, great bodies of the natives were just around the north-west point, about half a mile from us; the point hid them from us. We prepared ourselves, but they did not come; they were heard by the sentry at the back of the camp, and a jagged spear was found at daylight, supposed to have been thrown at the serjeant of marines who had been on alert near that spot, during the morning.

Sunday, July 8th.—At noon, a party, consisting of Lieutenant Carnac, three midshipmen, and twenty marines, accompanied by Dr. Wood, again made an excursion into the interior, in a more easterly direction than before, not having then succeeded in finding the source of the river. It was expected they would have been able to return by five or six o'clock at farthest but did not come in till two P.M. the following day, having lost their way, and broken their compass. Guns were fired from the Success, at intervals, during the day and night, none of which were heard by them. Native dogs were in numbers in the camp this night, but as they appeared harmless, I directed they might not be molested.

Monday, July 9th.—Captain Stirling announced his intention of leaving the bay in a fortnight. The heavy logs being completed in the house, the framing of the upper part was commenced. The stockade far advanced. The 39th and volunteers employed in their huts; the marines in erecting a fence, to enclose the camp. No interruption during the night.

Wednesday, July 11th.—I have not, as yet, seen any stone likely to be serviceable, nor are there shells, in any quantities, for the purpose of making lime. The coast is composed of hardened clay, and conglomerate, and towards the interior strongly impregnated, with iron ... (Smyth, 1827 diary).

The Aborigines were not seen then for three days. The *Success* spent the day and night firing signal cannons, so perhaps they kept away because of the gun noise. But then, on Friday 13 July, a positive meeting occurred:

> ... *Working parties continued as usual. At seven, A.M. a party from the Success hauled their seine about a mile to the south-east, and on leaving the beach, eight or ten natives came down. I proceeded towards them with Lieutenant Belcher, of the Success, directing the whole of the remainder of our party to retire to camp. With some difficulty, we prevailed on them to allow us to come up to them with some fish, biscuit and a few other trifles: the extraordinary jealous caution they maintained induces me to think they have, more than probably, been dealt treacherously with by the Malays, of whose visits, on all the small islands contiguous to the main land (but not on it), there are many evident proofs, such as places for boiling trepang ... These natives were armed with spears, three or four each, some of them jaggard; one was pointed with iron, perhaps a part of the plunder of our whaleboat. We gave them what few things we had, and, in return, the chief presented me with a small purse, suspended from his neck, containing shells, neatly netted, and with much the same mesh used by us. We left them much more composed, and, as far as signs could be understood, with a promise to return to-morrow at the same time. Night passed tranquilly ... (Smyth, 1827 diary).*

Dr Duncan recorded the same event, (although dated his entry 11 July, rather than 13 July), and it is from him that we learn that two men, Mariac and Iacama earned their nicknames, 'Wellington' and 'Waterloo':

> ... *On the 11th, at about ten, A.M. seven of the natives came down on the beach, near the Lagoon, carrying their spears. Captain Smyth and Mr. Belcher went up to them and gave them some articles; two of them, who were named Wellington and Waterloo, came into the settlement along with them—they were bedaubed over with red clay. After eating some biscuit, &c. they joined their companions, and returned into the woods.*
>
> *Whilst the two chiefs remained in the camp, the other five natives stood at a short distance, with their spears in their hands (Duncan, 1827).*

An unidentified 'gentleman' who wrote to the *Sydney Gazette* held strong views on these men:

The Chief got the name of Wellington from Captain Smyth, which he retains. He is the most savage fellow of the tribe; not one of us likes him; his Chief Officer was called Waterloo by Smyth, which name he also retains. (Gazette, 18 June 1828)

Smyth seems to have returned to his diary several times during Saturday 14 July, updating it with momentous events concerning an improving relationship with the Iwaidja:

Saturday, July 14th.—At eleven A.M., eighteen of the natives came down to the fishing beach, about a mile from us. The surgeon, Mr. Belcher, and myself, went to them with some biscuit, and a few other little presents; they were much pleased, but still observed a vigilant and distrustful caution, and remained but a short time. Three P.M.—Two of the native chiefs have been in my tent and are now on board the Success. Four P.M.—Returned, much gratified with dresses given them on board, and gone to their tribe: this circumstance, I hope, will entirely put a stop to their nocturnal visits. While they were near my tent, close to which the wrecked boat, and the recovered rope-jack (which was found buried in the mud) were lying; neither of them appeared to notice the one or the other. I did not think it necessary to remind them of these circumstances in so early an acquaintance. They are generally strong, muscular men, infinitely more so than the description of natives in the neighbourhood of Sydney. Some of them were daubed over from the crown of the head to the ancle [sic] with a kind of pipe clay. No disturbance this night ...

There were clearly many people in the surrounding area at the time, and curiosity as well as fear was evident:

... Sunday, July 15th.—Seven of the natives came into the camp, and were fed, and shown over the place. Much surprise was manifested by them, and particularly when I showed them the use of the gun, by bringing down two large hawks, of which there are vast numbers. The power of pistols also astonished them, and they begged we would not use them again, as it gave them great pain in the head. Mr. Belcher and myself, wishing to show we had every confidence in them, went with them and joined their party of about twenty, at a distance of about three miles to the S.S.E., near the beach. We afterwards hailed the jollyboat of the Success, with Mr. Carr and four midshipmen in her, and with two of

44

the chiefs got in, and went across the bay to the west, about five
miles, where they gave us to understand was their great place of
assembly. After getting on shore, about thirty, with spears, made
their appearance; but, by order of their chief, laid them down,
and approached us with most extraordinary attitudes and gestures.
They were eager to lead us to their place of general rendezvous,
and we followed them for about two miles on a well-beaten track;
but as the sun was near down, and one or two instances of daring
theft had taken place, I thought it prudent not to go further; and,
to the evident disappointment and displeasure of the sable group,
we returned to our boat. The two who were left as a guard in her
had been strongly entreated to follow us into the wood, which
induces me to think they had in view the pilfering of the boat
at parting. They presented us with a spear, which we understood
as a token of friendship. The bones, and three or four skulls, on
the beach, engaged our attention, but they showed signs of great
displeasure at our approaching them, and we desisted. The night
passed perfectly tranquil ... (Smyth, 1827 diary).

Dr Duncan, of the *Success*, also recorded a version of events:

... On the 15th, seven or eight of them came down, with the two
who were on board the Success: they remained only for a short
time; in the afternoon a party went out sailing, they landed on
the opposite shore, in a sandy bay, where the natives had often
been seen. Their canoes were on the beach. On the approach of
the boat, several of the natives appeared, and made signs to our
people to go on shore, which desire they complied with. There were
several human bones lying on the sands, but the natives did not
wish our men to touch them, but made signs to the men to follow
them into the woods, which they did for a short distance; but
being unarmed, and some of the natives making rather too free,
they thought it most prudent to return. Whilst in the woods with
the natives, one of them stole a handkerchief from our Lieutenant.
On Wellington knowing of the theft, he immediately made the
man return it. It was then offered to Wellington, but he would not
accept of it until they returned to the beach ... (Duncan, 1827).

This looked like a promising start for cross-cultural relationships,
but two days later, things started to go sour, following the theft of an
axe:

... Tuesday, July 17th.—The natives (twelve) came into the

45

camp, and were given biscuit, &c. One assisted in blowing the forge; another in scrubbing the hammocks of the Success. I was anxious to establish a perfect good understanding with them and did not check it. Early in the afternoon, they left us, and went two miles at least along the beach, in our sight, when two of them (the leaders, Wellington and Waterloo and to whom we had been particularly kind,) struck into the wood, came up to a party cutting wood, and, remaining a few minutes, seized on an axe, and ran off. Two soldiers followed them near to their general assembly, when a large body came out with spears, and with much difficulty the soldiers escaped. This night, they again began their marauding system in the early part of the night; it was dark, but the guard heard them in all directions round the camp. I considered their faithless conduct did not deserve lenity, and I ordered the several sentries to fire whenever they approached. One shot was fired, and no more was heard of them ... (Smyth, 1827 diary).

Smyth was offended greatly when his tokens of friendship were so treacherously repaid by dishonest thievery. He was now in no mood for conciliation, although some 'officers of the *Success*' didn't know this:

... Thursday, July 19th.—The natives were more bold last night and came into the forge. A shot was fired at them, and they disappeared. Tools and everything are carefully put out of their reach each night.

Friday, July 20th.—Two of the natives, the men who had stolen the axe, had the assurance to come into camp. Unfortunately, some officers of the Success received them in a friendly manner: it was my intention to have handcuffed one of them until his comrade brought in the stolen axe; however, I merely showed my displeasure at their conduct, and ordered them out of the camp to fetch it. At a few yards distance, one of them, with a look of expressive contempt of me, took up a frock from the ground, and away they both started, in the face of the whole camp. A pursuit took place, but they ran too fast for us. The frock, however, was dropped in the flight ... (Smyth, 1827 diary).

A few days later, Private James Taylor made a mistake. On 28 July, he joined several others fishing a little along the coast from the fort. The fishing party were under strict instructions to stick together but Taylor, either foolishly or through ill-advised bravado, especially when considering the ongoing trouble with some of the Iwaidja, left his colleagues early to return home. A lone man following the coast was an easy target, and 50 or 60 Iwaidja tribesmen delighted in his discovery. Taylor was terrified and ran for his life. Spears were thrown, and one talented marksman was rewarded by seeing his spear enter Taylor's back, as he ran. Fear is a great motivator; Taylor pressed on and made it to the fort, bloodied but not fatally injured. Dr Wood was able to remove the spear which

> ... had entered near the Spine and had perforated the lungs;
> the Spear was jagged and the 4 jags, extracted from the wound,
> were 2 of them broken and incomplete; whether the bits broken
> off them were in or out of the wound Doctor Wood could not
> ascertain; great suppuration has been carried on, and at one
> period the man appeared to be recovering, Wound healed, but he
> has relapsed, and daily getting worse with great debility, pain in
> his lungs, difficulty of breathing, etc ... (Smyth, 1827a)

Taylor was taken to Melville Island in October and returned to Sydney with other invalids on the *Governor Phillip*. Lieutenant Coke wrote that they were 'reduced to skeletons and cripples' (Connor, 2002).

The Iwaidja revelled in their success. Captain Smyth reported that a settlers' fishing party had met a group of tribesmen, who delighted in re-enacting the spearing, pointing to each other's backs and taunting the fishermen. This same group set fire to the grass the settlement had been harvesting for their cattle and as thatch for their huts. Smyth was livid. Not only were the Iwaidja resisting his settlement, they were mocking the settlers. He decided to go to war. On 30 July, Smyth ordered one of the carronades to fire 'grapeshot' at a group of Iwaidja in what was the second time a cannon had been fired against Aboriginal people in New Holland (Connor, 2002). The Iwaidja scattered, in awe of the noise and the unknown technology. A party of 13 soldiers were sent out in a hunting party and an Iwaidja 'was shot,' Smyth reported to Governor Darling, 'and several (were) reported to be severely wounded' (Smyth, 1827b). Encouraged by their success, Smyth then sent the soldiers out on several other occasions, in different directions, but they didn't capture anyone.

The Iwaidja, not surprisingly, withdrew, and were not seen for several weeks. The settlers slept more easily at night, but not for long, as they were again affronted by the Aborigines, one October night, when they managed to steal a small boat from its mooring, despite there being at least two sentries within a few metres. It was another daring act of war, thought Smyth, and again the Iwaidja had come up trumps.

The commandant desperately sought an answer to the Iwaidja problem. The wet season had now arrived, and heavy rains fell most afternoons, and the bush quickly thickened with its annual growth. If only Smyth could talk with these people, calm everyone down …

Just after Christmas in 1827, he had an idea. He offered his men five pounds reward for whomever could catch an Aborigine or two. They would be kept prisoner in the fort until they learned to speak English and they would then be able to translate for the Englishmen, and, once communication was possible, peace would follow. Major Campbell had tried to do something similar at Fort Dundas, although his prisoner, a man named Tambu, had managed to escape from the underground powder store where he was kept, before learning any English. Dr Gold was killed soon after, perhaps in revenge for Tambu's abduction (Pugh, 2017).

Despite Campbell's failure, on the afternoon of 27 December, Smyth selected a party of three soldiers (Privates Thomas Smith, John Norton and Charles Miller, all of the 39th), and two Crown Prisoner volunteers (Henry Adams, and James Murray), and ordered them to hunt and capture an Iwaidja person. With them was Poalo Sois, the Lascar Lieutenant Hicks had rescued in the Gulf of Carpentaria after his ship was wrecked. He was the only one of the party without a musket and bayonet. Smyth noted his orders in his diary:

*... Six Men Volunteering to go in quest of our annoying and
dangerous Neighbours the Blacks, and if possible to bring in one
for me to keep as an hostage to their future better behaviour, I
gave them permission with Instructions for their guidance and,
should their Situation render any Violence necessary, to be careful
and guard against any Women of Children they might see ...
(Smyth HRA V6 p811, 1828).*

The party were out for several hours before they found some
Aborigines. About 4 p.m., three people were seen paddling a small
canoe along the coast. The hunters carefully followed them, hidden
behind the front line of vegetation on the beach. Incredibly, they
remained unobserved, even when they sneaked onto the sand to look
for footprints or other signs of people. Once, they found two old
campfires and the tracks of many people and their dogs.

Carefully, they continued to follow the canoeists. The sun
set, but the waxing moon, six days before full, lit their path well.
After several hours, a cluster of campfires shone through the bush
ahead, and they could hear distant voices and laughter. They quietly
worked out a plan of attack. It meant sneaking around the back of
some dark mangrove trees, where they were thick. The path was sandy
and clear, so they made no noise, and the Iwaidja were calm anyway,
not expecting any trouble. Even their dogs remained unaware of the
hunting party. Then the cover of the trees suddenly ran out and they
were in full view of a group of about 60 people, sitting or standing
round their fires. Many were asleep. There was a shout.

Henry Adams, a 40-year-old convict brick maker, was the
first to be spotted. The warriors leapt for their spears, and several
went flying in Henry's direction. Suddenly, fearful for their own
lives, the soldiers attacked, firing three muskets at the Aborigines,
keeping two in reserve whilst they reloaded. There was chaos. People
ran, terrified, but on hearing no more shots, started gathering their
forces. Then the soldiers fired the remaining muskets and most of
the Iwaidja then headed bush to take shelter. Four or five of them
struggled with gunshot wounds. Henry Adams loaded and fired his

musket several more times to keep them away, whilst the others tried to capture some prisoners. Privates Thomas Smith and Charles Miller and the other convict volunteer, James Murray, managed to drive a few people into the water. One of them, a woman large enough to be mistaken for a man in the moonlight, carried two children towards the canoes. There was a struggle. The convict bayonetted her, and she slipped beneath the water. When the soldiers returned to the fires, the men carried two children. One was already dead, shot in the belly, but the other, a little girl of about 6 years, was still alive, although wounded in her side. She was their only prisoner and the prize of the bounty hunters, now keen to collect their £5 reward.

Henry Adams saw a man on his hands and knees near the fires. He was badly wounded with his intestines spilling from his belly. The soldiers took pity on him. Charles Miller said

> ... we endeavoured to see if he was in a fit state to be brought to the Settlement; but, finding that the Intestines were protruding from his Belly, we thought it better to put him out of his misery at once and he was accordingly dispatch ... (HRA, 1827c).

Private Miller found the axe that had been stolen from the fort by Wellington and Waterloo several weeks before. Then, realising what they had done, the hunting party became nervous—perhaps there'd be a reprisal. Miller quickly used the axe to break every spear the Iwaidja had left behind to ensure they would remain unarmed, and they took their prize, a very frightened, injured little girl, back to the fort, arriving just before dawn. She was carried by Paolo Sois, because he was unarmed.

This extraordinary raid made waves. A Court of Inquiry was held by Smyth, and all the participants were interviewed, except Paolo Sois (because he spoke 'English language very unintelligibly'), about their actions that night. Adams was asked if he knew how the little girl had been wounded:

> ... 'I do not', he said, 'but I imagine the unfortunate woman and her children were all wounded by the first three shots that were

fired. They were in a cluster around the fire. My gun was loaded with slugs and I levelled low in order to disable those I might hit, and afterwards to take them prisoners. The child was also on or near the spot in the direction which I had fixed when they made their flight as I then saw it standing there … (HRA, 1827c).

Captain Smyth wrote to Colonial Secretary MacLeay, in February, explaining why the woman had been killed:

… Volunteer James Murray… endeavoured to take the woman and child prisoners; she was a very large and powerful woman. She made desperate resistance, rushed into the water, and he gave her a wound with the bayonet; this he certainly should not have done had he been certain it was a woman; but fearing that an escape would be made, he was determined if possible, to secure the person. The children were afterwards brought on shore, one was dead and the other was slightly wounded; the woman fell and he supposed died in the water … (Smyth, 12 February 1828).

Despite the horror of the encounter, Smyth was later pleased.

… Not a native has been seen, heard of or traced since that period. If it has the effect of keeping them perfectly aloof, I have every reason to believe that the preservation of the lives of some of His Majesty's Subjects has been effected … (Smyth, 12 February 1828).

Inexplicably, Governor Darling mostly sat on his hands over this incident, which he described as 'reprehensible and disgraceful'. Darling asked for a 'secret and confidential' report (reproduced in Appendix 2), from Smyth, which he wrote from Emu Plains near Sydney, in August 1828, but no one was ever charged of any crime because 'His Excellency has deemed it unadvisable to take any Public Notice of the matter at the present moment' (MacLeay, 14 August 1828).

Henry Adams was awarded his ticket-of-leave in May 1830, and his freedom in 1834, after his term of sentence expired. He died in Wee Waa, NSW, in 1857. James Murray, who had earned a seven year stretch for stealing calico, was freed almost immediately after his return to Sydney, on the *Ann,* at the end of his sentence, in March 1829. He had demanded Smyth give him his freedom a month early because it was, he said, always given to prisoners convicted in Ireland, and then, when Smyth refused, he stopped work. This earned him 3 weeks in the guard house on bread, flour and meat only, while he waited for the *Ann* to depart (Smyth, 1827a). He died in Camperdown, NSW, twenty-four years later.

The three soldiers, Miller, Adams and Norton returned to Sydney with their Regiment in 1829 and were posted to Madras in 1832.

The little girl recovered from her wounds and settled into the fort life quite quickly. She was renamed Mary Waterloo Raffles because Smyth thought she resembled the man he called Waterloo and there was a chance she might be his daughter. Some of the hunting party incorrectly thought the man whom they'd 'dispatched' from his misery, also looked like Waterloo. They were, however, also sure he was the same man who had speared James Taylor in the back the previous July, but this seems unlikely.

On Wednesday, 16 April, the brig *Philip Dundas* arrived with Dr Robert Davis aboard, as well as a further detachment of soldiers from the 39th, and stores and livestock: '4 head of Cattle, (1 Bull and 3 Cows), 11 Sheep and 94 birds: Turkeys, Ducks and Fowls'.

The next day, as they were unloading the *Philip Dundas*, another brig arrived, the *Governor Phillip*[*]. This ship carried Captain Humphrey Hartley, the new commandant of Fort Dundas with men of the 57th Regiment. She also brought the replacement surgeon for the murdered Dr Gold: Dr William Sherwin, Surgeon, and Lieutenant George Sleeman of the 39th Regiment, unaware he was about to become commandant.

Captain Smyth was suffering from scurvy, and with two doctors in the fort, he quickly arranged to have them both examine him. Doctors Davis and Sherwin were in agreement and were able to give him a medical certificate that relieved him of his duty at Fort Wellington:

---

[*] *His Majesty's Ship Governor Phillip* was a 177-ton government brig built in 1821. She was sunk on 5 November 1848, after hitting a reef off Gull Island in the Furneaux Group, with the loss of 16 crew and passengers. Sixty-nine others were saved (*The Moreton Bay Courier* 16 Dec 1848).

MEDICAL CERTIFICATE. Raffles Bay, 18 April 1828.

THIS is to Certify that we have carefully Examined Captain Henry Smyth of the 39th Regt. and have found that he has laboured under Scurvy and now suffers from Anasarca of his lower Extremities and prostration of appetite, apparently produced by too great bodily and mental exertion; and we do believe that his removal to Head Quarters will be essentially necessary for the Reestablishment of his Health, as this climate does not appear to us likely to effect that desirable Result.

ROBERT M. DAVIS, M.D., Ass. Surgn 39th regiment,
WILLIAM SHERWIN, Surgeon (Smyth, 12 February 1828)

Smyth was relieved at last, just as another officer, Lieutenant Sleeman had arrived. He could leave Sleeman in charge of Fort Wellington!

Arrangements were made and Smyth sailed from Raffles Bay in the *Governor Phillip* on 24 April 1828. He had worked just 10 months in the north. There were 13 other passengers on board, also invalids, who had been relieved by the doctors.

The *Governor Phillip* went first to Melville Island and, whilst there, Smyth asked Major Campbell to send a gardener to Fort Wellington. Campbell wrote:

... On Captain Smyth's arrival from Raffles Bay, he represented to me that that Settlement sustained great loss from the want of a Gardner. I had only one man who was at all capable of attending to a garden besides the Government Gardner, and, as this man had been assistant gardener for two years, had conducted himself well and bore a Ticket of leave, I thought he would be a proper person to send down. I therefore sent him and recommended the Commandant, Lieut. Sleeman, to give him the same allowances as were granted to ticket of leave men on Melville Island, until he had communicated on the subject to Headquarters. The name of this Prisoner is Michael McCarthy ... (Campbell to Mackay HRA 20 June 1828).

McCarthy's success in the gardens over the next twelve months was integral to the improved health of the settlers[*].

---

[*] McCarthy prospered and earned his ticket-of-leave in Sydney in 1830. He lived in Liverpool and died there in 1865, aged fifty-nine years.

Unfortunately, the negative reports on the health and privations experienced by the early settlers were, at the same time, reaching government ears in Sydney and London. The delays due to distance meant information was already up to six months old by the time it reached either end.

Captain Smyth returned to Sydney and was living at Emu Plains a few months later. He recovered well from his bout of scurvy, and Colonial Secretary MacLeay met with him in early July. Smyth was ordered to write an account of the fort in the time between his final official dispatch from Raffles Bay and his departure on 24 April. He did this by sending MacLeay extracts from his diary and offered advice from his experience that would improve the success of the settlement (this letter is reproduced in Appendix 2).

Captain Smyth went on to serve as commandant at Port Macquarie from November 1828 until 5 July 1832, on an annual salary of £200[*] (Almanac, 1830). He was a bachelor (or a widower, if indeed he was the Captain *Smith* who arrived on the *Earl St Vincent* on 13 August 1826), despite a requirement that commandants of distant settlements should, if possible, be married men and have their families with them[†]. He was a sometimes 'lax' and gentle commandant who was well liked, as were his predecessors, because Port Macquarie never built a harsh reputation in any of its 11 years of operation as a convict settlement from 1820. One achievement he was known for was having a wooden floor constructed in the part of the church used for Port Macquarie's first schoolhouse, because the flagstones were too cold for the children's feet (Rogers, 1982).

---

[*] On Commandant Smyth's staff in Port Macquarie was Stephen Partridge (1792–1878), as Superintendent of Convicts and Public Works, on an annual salary of £100 (Uptin, 1957). Partridge arrived in NSW in 1814 with the 46th Regiment, went on both of Oxley's explorations and later took out licence No. 1 for a pub (the 'New Inn') in Port Macquarie. He married his convict servant, Julia Cotterdown from Bantry Bay in Ireland. They are not part of this story except through their connection with Smyth, but they were my great X7 grandparents (Uptin, 1957).

[†] In fact, none of the commandants of the two 1820s settlements appear to have been married men.

Port Macquarie became a free town in 1831, and Smyth oversaw the redistribution of the Crown Prisoners. Those who could not be reassigned in New South Wales were sent to Moreton Bay and Smyth recommended that their destination remain a secret for as long as possible: 'The general dread of Moreton Bay was such that many would take to the bush if they knew their destination' he wrote.

Eighteen months after the convicts were sent away, Smyth was replaced by a civilian governor. He left reluctantly, showing poor grace, and humiliated the incoming civilian Governor and his family by sour and non-welcoming behaviour (Annabel, et al., 2003), but he needed to re-join his regiment in any case. The 39th left New South Wales for Madras in India on 21 July 1832, and as they left, Governor Darling presented the Regiment with new colours and paid the men many compliments: the official inspection report stated that it was "a good body of men, well-appointed and in very good order" (White, 1955). Apart from Fort Wellington, soldiers of the 39th had seen service guarding Crown Prisoners and establishing settlements in Hobart, Sydney, Newcastle, Bathurst, and Norfolk Island. They also helped establish the Swan River colony in Fremantle/Perth.

Three of the regiment died at sea before reaching Australia (BDA, 2019), and several more died whilst on duty in Australia (Rootsweb, 2019) but, in India, the Regiment fared even more poorly. Cholera broke out among them in 1833, and the regiment lost Dr Robert Davis (1798–1839), who had served at both Fort Wellington and King George's Sound (Mulvaney & Green, 1992), Captain Thomas Meyrich, a 22 year veteran, four sergeants, 42 rank and file, two wives, and 11 children, in a five week period (Cannon, 1853).

Smyth sailed with the regiment to India and performed admirably with the 'Eastern Column' in Sudapore. In 1834, his commander in India, Lieutenant-Colonel G.M. Steuart, reported that Smyth was severely wounded in action, although not dangerously:

... Since the first day of operations I have been deprived of the services of Captain Smyth, of His Majesty's 39th Regiment, who, although severely

wounded in the foot, continued to lead on his men throughout the day,
after forcing passage of the river ... (Steuart, 19 Sept 1834).

Despite this wound and the scourge of cholera killing many of his colleagues, Smyth made it back to England safely, and he next appears in the records as a witness for the Select Committee on Military Spending (Papers, 4 August 1835) in London. His answers to questions posed by the Select Committee show his concern for his men at Fort Wellington. The Committee asked him to compare how hard a soldier's life was in New South Wales with elsewhere. Smyth told them of the number of nights of disturbed rest they had at Fort Wellington, where the soldiers never had two nights in bed in a row due to sentry duties, and said that it was hard work compared to other roles. He also supported the commissariat officers, of whom the Committee were critical—believing them to be overstaffed and underworked. Smyth argued that 'the commissariat have to supply an immense number, the troops and convicts together' and believed they 'economically conducted with reference to the public service'. The only instance he had that was worthy of complaint about the commissariat, during his time at Port Raffles, was a cargo of 'some very indifferent salt meat' (Committee, 4 August 1835).

Captain Smyth's ultimate fate is unknown, but he is remembered in the Northern Territory in the naming of Smyth Road, in Howard Springs.

Chapter 4
Lieutenant George Sleeman

Lieutenant George Sleeman, and a 30-man detachment of the 39th Regiment, brought 194 convicts from Ireland under guard on the *Countess of Harcourt*, arriving in Sydney on 25 July 1827. It was the first posting for the ambitious lieutenant, who received his promotion on 5 January 1826, in Ireland, after having been forced to remain on half pay for 12 years until a full-time posting came up (a common event in post-war England).

On arrival in Sydney the 39th needed a celebration:

> *... The Guard, consisting of part of the Grenadier Company and battalion of the 39th regiment under orders of Lieut. George Sleeman and Ensign Spencer were disembarked in the afternoon and marched to their quarters in the military barracks, through George Street, preceded by bugles, drums, and fifes, playing the regimental welcome. The military detachment was marched from their barracks during the afternoon of Monday, towards Woolloomooloo Bay at the head of which a general halt was made. For better than an hour afterwards, the soldiers kept up an almost incessant fire upon two targets, which were set up at no great distance from the water's edge. When they had riddled and knocked about the targets, till they could no longer stand upright, the detachment retreated to barracks ... (Australian, 29 June 1927).*

Sleeman was interested in the position of commandant of the penal colony at King George's Sound in Western Australia where

---

* The *Countess of Harcourt* was the ship used to deliver convicts and members of the 3rd Regiment of Foot to Fort Dundas in 1824.

Albany now stands, and he requested the role several times but, instead, was posted to Raffles Bay as second in charge to Smyth. He arrived on the colonial brig *Governor Phillip* on 17 April 1828.

It was the right position to be in if anything happened to the commandant, and he didn't have to wait long: Doctor Davis and Doctor Sherwin, who had both arrived at the same time, diagnosed Commandant Smyth as a sufferer of scurvy. Smyth was probably delighted: scurvy may have been an uncomfortable inconvenience, but it gave him the excuse he needed to leave the north.

On 24 April, Smyth left Raffles Bay and Sleeman became the acting commandant of Fort Wellington. He seems to have had mixed feelings about the role. Although he was now commandant, his first despatch to Colonial Secretary MacLeay, two days before his temporary appointment began, ends with a plea to be relieved from the post as soon as possible. This was made particularly poignant because the only other officer in the settlement, potentially Sleeman's only company, was Dr Davis, and the two men disliked each other intensely. Sleeman's ambition was still aimed at the settlement in King George's Sound, and it seemed the community in Fort Wellington was to again suffer the administration of an officer who did not want to be there, despite the promise of his 'utmost effort':

Sir, Fort Wellington, Raffles Bay, 22nd April 1828.

I have the honor to acquaint you, for the information Arrival of His Excellency the Governor, that I arrived at this settlement in His Majesty's Colonial brig, Governor Phillip on Thursday the 17th Instant; and that I had the satisfaction of disembarking, on the following day, all the men who came with me in the possession of good health ...

I sincerely regret that the serious injury which Captain Smyth's health has sustained from his residence here, will oblige him to avail himself of His Excellency's permission to return to Head Quarters; an event, the necessity for which I am assured will be deeply lamented by all those who compose this infant Colony, over whose interests he has been so unceasingly watchful, and to each of whom he has extended many individual acts of kindness. As he

*will, on his arrival at Sydney, communicate to the Governor the
most minute and detailed particulars of everything connected with
this Settlement, I fear His Excellency would consider it premature
in me to offer an Opinion on so important a subject, and with so
imperfect a knowledge ... My utmost efforts shall be directed to
the promotion of the interests of this Settlement in every way as
long as it may please His Excellency to continue me in charge of it;
but I shall feel extremely grateful if His Excellency will permit me,
when convenient, to proceed to relieve Captain Wakefield at King
George's Sound.*

*I have, &c, GEORGE SLEEMAN, Lieut., 39th Regt. (Sleeman,
1828).*

Sleeman's four months in charge of Fort Wellington were short
but, to his credit, he really did do his utmost to improve the settlement,
as he promised. His second dispatch, in June, was 3000 words long,
and notwithstanding the high use of platitudes for his audience, it
covered a wide range of topics relating to the settlement. For example:

*... My attention has been principally directed, since I came
here, to hastening the erection of the Cottage which Captain
Smyth had projected as a residence for the Commandant, the
foundation of which was dug before he left; but I have departed
from his Plan and have substituted the Enclosed (drawn by H.
Langton, principal Overseer) for His Excellency's approval ...
the Cottage will be adapted for the residence of two officers, and
will be completed with just the same Labour and expense as if it
had been built as it was first intended, and I think it will now be
much more convenient and handsome. It is situated on the most
Elevated ground near the Settlement, and commands an extensive
and beautiful view of the bay, Island and adjacent scenery ... All
the Wood used in building this Cottage will be put together in
such a way as to admit of its being taken to pieces and removed, if
required ... (Sleeman, 1828).*

This cottage was built on the headland—the highest point of
the coast where, Sleeman suggested, the fort itself should have been
sited. In fact, he was so keen on the higher site, and so critical of the
site chosen by Captain Stirling that he felt it his duty to design a new
fort:

... it would have been a much better situation for a Fort than the present one, which scarcely deserves the name, being situated on a bank of Sand not more than five feet above the level of the Sea at high water at Spring tides ...

The situation of the Settlement is injudiciously chosen for strength or convenience; but, should His Excellency be pleased to continue it, I have presumed to enclose a plan of a Fort (drawn by H. Langton) which could be erected with little trouble and equally trifling expense and which would bid defiance to any hostile attempts of the Natives ...

Sleeman didn't trust the natives, but he didn't trust the Macassan fishermen either, whom Smyth had been at pains to build friendly relationships with. The new fort would also:

... guard against the insidious, cunning and hollow friendship of the Malays, who most probably will resort hither in future in great numbers. This Fort would enclose a Barrack, Guard house, Magazine and Engineer's Stores, and be built on a natural elevation of thirty feet above the Sea ... (Sleeman, 1828).

Sleeman's antagonism seems strange because he met neither the Macassan fishermen, nor any Aborigines. The settlement wasn't visited by Macassans during his time in command because it was the wrong time of year, and the only Aborigines who appeared were four indistinct figures seen at a distance in July, on the other side of the bay, and a couple more who were near the fort in late August, but who quickly disappeared into the bush when challenged. Sleeman was in no mood to offer friendship, anyway. He suspected the two came:

... with the view ... of pilfering what they could find; but, having been three times challenged and fired at by the Sentry, they decamped without giving further trouble ...

The leaking *Mary Elizabeth*, under Lieutenant Hicks, made a run to Koepang in Timor, to buy supplies (at a cost of £93 14s 8d) for Fort Wellington in January 1828, but she was outliving her usefulness. Smyth found her a drain on his manpower, and Sleeman claimed that the crew ate more supplies than she had provided to the settlement. With Captain Hartley on Melville Island in agreement,

Sleeman then sent Lieutenant Hicks, now a widower*, and the *Mary Elizabeth* back to Sydney. Sleeman mollified the dismissal by being:

> ... *induced to order the issue of eight Gallons of Rum from the Commissariat Stores here to him and the Crew of that Ship, with a clear understanding that the amount of it should be deducted from the Wages due to them on their return to Sydney should His Excellency the Governor be pleased so to direct ... (Sleeman, 1828).*

On board with Hicks was Oodeen, the Ceylonese interpreter. A family man, he was at Fort Wellington without his family, which now included five children. The first trepang season was over and he was at a loose end with no interpreting to do, so Sleeman granted him leave to return to Sydney to pick them up. Unfortunately, by the time he arrived, his wife had already found transport north for her and the children, and they passed each other en-route. Poor Oodeen then had to negotiate a speedy return back to Fort Wellington before being reunited with them (Clark, 2013).

In September *HMS Satellite*† under Captain John Laws, dropped anchor in the bay on the first of its two visits. Sleeman was able to send his third and final dispatch to MacLeay. In it, he boasted that the cottage, which Barker later also mentioned, had 15,000 shingles:

> ... *The Cottage intended for the residence of the Commandant is nearly finished, having a substantial roof covered with good Shingles cut out of the Stringy bark and being very neatly Weatherboarded with a Whitish Yellow wood, very similar to and apparently as durable as the Moreton bay pine; this Wood can be procured in great abundance a few miles from the Settlement and is easily converted into any useful purpose. The Cottage, which is a commodious building, is entirely built of it and reflects great credit on the few men who have been employed in erecting it. A firm and neat railing has also been put round it, leaving a Square of forty feet from the building: the Windows, doors and the interior work remain to be completed which, with the few artificers we have, will take some time to accomplish ... (Sleeman, 1828).*

---

* His wife, Sophie, died in childbirth at Fort Dundas.

† Captain John Laws R.N. Laws prepared a report on the two settlements which is reproduced in Appendix 3.

The weather had been so good over the dry season, and everyone was so healthy that Sleeman increased the work hours for the 19 convict volunteers by an hour a day. They were apparently pleased with this ... according to Sleeman, it was:

> ... a measure which they most readily and willingly complied with; indeed, their conduct has been with two or three exceptions most orderly and becoming ... (Sleeman, 1828).

Sleeman always wrote well of the men, waxing lyrically on their good behaviour, and going so far as to reward them:

> ... The General good conduct of the Soldiers and the Prisoners of the Crown since my arrival here, and the cheerfulness and alacrity which the former have shewn in the discharge of their duty and the latter in the execution of their labour, has induced me with the advice of the Surgeon to avail myself of His Excellency's permission to order the issue of one seventh of an ounce of Tobacco daily to each of these individuals ... (Sleeman, 1828).

Sleeman put a lot of energy into expanding and improving the gardens. As long as there is water enough for the plants, the northern dry season is an excellent growing time for fruit and vegetables that may cope less well in the wet season. With the arrival of Michael McCarthy*, the gardener sent from Fort Dundas at Smyth's request, and the appointment of a full-time soldier to work in the gardens, there was soon good food and a great improvement in the health of the community. Sleeman mentioned a soldier suffering from dysentery and two convicts still with a touch of scurvy, but for one six-week period the hospital had no patients at all. The problem of poor health appeared to have been solved. In June, Sleeman was satisfied that:

> ... it will become a productive and valuable Garden, as good pumpkins, Melons, Bringel, etc., have already been produced, and Yams, Custard Apple, Lemon, Citron, Sugar Cane, Arrow root, Tamarisk, Ginger, Maize, Pomelo, the Cotton tree and other plants look healthy and I think will answer well; I have had many useful Vegetables planted, amongst which were some Potatoes;

---

* Sleeman paid Michael McCarthy, gardener for the settlement, a salary of 'two shillings and two pence per diem, one shilling of which' was 'daily deducted for his rations and credited to Government'.

but this is not the proper season for sowing seed, and the land is therefore preparing until it arrives ... (Sleeman, 1828).

And in September

... a good supply of useful Vegetables will no doubt next season be procured, and the adjacent land, which has been cleared of Wood, etc., will in all probability yield a good Crop of Maize, the season for sowing of which is near at hand. The small quantity of Sugar Cane, which grew in the garden and which was healthy and good, was scarcely sufficient to allow of a trial being made of its quality. I therefore had it cut and transplanted, and it is now doing well. Some Pineapple plants lately received from Melville Island have also been put in the garden and look healthy; indeed I think the soil is capable of producing anything which the Climate will allow ... (Sleeman, 1828).

Sleeman also had the stock yards rebuilt and a fence around the gardens made of slabs of timber from stringy bark trees. He was interested in finding out as much about the country as possible and sent samples of soil and timber to Sydney for analysis, on the *Mary Elizabeth*. He then explored some of the surroundings, including taking a boat trip eight kilometres up a local river, which he named after himself, until he could go no further due to log jams.

Sleeman's time was up quickly, as Captain Collet Barker arrived to take over on 13 September. He then achieved his ambition and sailed to King George's Sound to take over there as commandant, as he'd been planning for years. His time there was also short, less than a year, because he had to give way to Captain Collet Barker again, after the closure of Fort Wellington.

Whilst in charge of King George's Sound, Sleeman developed gardens, built a hospital and a grand commandant's house, and referred often to the good behaviour of his men, including the Crown Prisoners in his dispatches, but of the local Aborigines, the Minang, Sleeman showed no interest, just as he had in Raffles Bay.

Chapter 5

Captain Collet Barker

Collet Barker was born on 31 December 1784. Little is known about his early life but his parents, William, a skinner, and Sarah, were in businesses in Newbury (Mulvaney, 1993), London, and his close relatives were drapers, skinners, goldsmiths, iron merchants, and solicitors.

Barker joined the 39th Regiment in 1806, at the age of 21, paying £400 for the rank of ensign[*]. He subsequently earned an income of 4 shillings 8 pence per day. He fought with the regiment in Spain and the USA, before spending ten years in the occupational forces in France and Ireland. He earned a promotion by merit to lieutenant in Sicily but needed a bit of luck to go further. Promotion was based on vacancies arising, and only one lieutenant in the regiment had managed to purchase a captaincy in the 9 years after the Battle of Waterloo, and that was his Fort Wellington predecessor, Captain Henry Smyth, in 1824. Barker's turn came on 10 July 1825, just one month before he sailed for New Holland.

The 39th Regiment was sent to Port Jackson in 18 detachments, totalling just over 900 men. Barker travelled aboard the *Phoenix* in charge of a detachment of 29 troops guarding the Crown Prisoners. The *Phoenix* arrived in Sydney on 18 July 1828, and, within a month, Barker was sent north to take over from George Sleeman, at Fort Wellington.

---

[*] The rank of ensign was equivalent to today's second lieutenant.

Barker's journal of his eleven months at Raffles Bay, and most of the subsequent year at King George's Sound survives. His almost illegible writing was 'deciphered' in the 1980s by Mulvaney, Green and Street and published in 1992 in a book titled *Commandant of Solitude*, which is now rare and demands a high price in the second hand market (Mulvaney & Green, 1992). His journal exhibits well Barker's qualities and scientific interests. He was equally an administrator, field naturalist*, botanist and geologist, as well as a military leader, who was interested in his community's health and the welfare of those he managed. Much of the journal is mundane, telling us which pig was ill, or about how the calf had been stung by a wasp, how difficult it was to keep the buffaloes near the settlement, and of the successes in the gardens, such as when a custard apple ripened, or the time when Captain Laws' coconut shoots rose above the ground.

Barker was also outstanding as the only commandant at either of the northern settlements to have any interest at all in the local Aborigines. Everyone else considered them to be a 'perpetual menace', but Barker found them interesting. Many became friends, and Barker continued to learn from them, to the benefit of his community, despite his men's antagonism. Wilson found that Barker 'had a great deal of difficulty to contend with, in his method of treating the natives; as no other individual in the settlement could be brought to consider these poor beings in any other light than wild beasts' (Wilson, 1835).

On 13 September 1828, Barker arrived in Raffles Bay with ten soldiers of the 39th, 12 new volunteer convicts, 17 sheep[†] and 4 pigs. The first thing he did was to tour the settlement with Lieutenant Sleeman so he could 'reconnoitre the neighbourhood'. He found the buildings and the fort in need of repair, although many were better

---

*   Barker's journal is full of descriptions of the animals they found, including a luminous worm, velvet geckos, snakes, bandicoots, native cats, 'flying iguanas' (frill-necked lizards), shells, jellyfish etc.

†   Most of the sheep Barker brought were dead within a fortnight. If a sheep died without the men meaning it to, they would still eat it only if it still bled when they reached it and the doctor approved, otherwise it would be fed to the pigs and dogs.

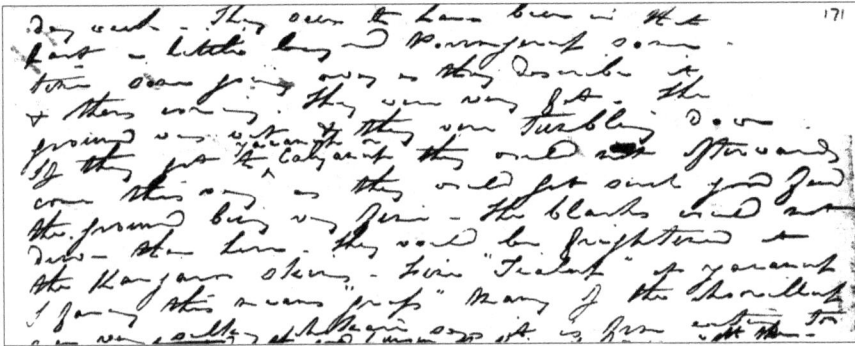

Figure 8: A section of Barker's journal. Its near illegibility restricted access to historians for many years (Mulvaney & Green, 1992).

than he'd expected, but the garden was 'miserable' with 'nothing in it worth speaking of'. This seems an exaggeration that denies the good work done during Sleeman's time as commandant: scurvy was all but gone and, within two or three weeks, the lime trees and bananas were flowering and custard apples fruiting, so they must have been doing well already. Sweet potatoes were also being grown on nearby Wood's Island and were also doing very well, and pumpkins were regularly harvested; at one time 50 were picked and distributed among the community.

For a few days, after Barker's arrival, the convicts' time was spent mostly in unloading the *Governor Phillip* and organising the supplies, so that the ship could leave. Doctor Davis collected 10 soldiers with signs of scurvy and sent them back to Sydney. All of them had arrived with Smyth at the beginning of the settlement and some were 'very weakly & unfit for the place'. Others were chosen to travel with Sleeman to King George's Sound. Four convicts were also sent south. Everyone else was well:

> ... I have great pleasure in reporting that I found the Settlement
> in a very healthy state. They have latterly had the benefit of the
> most favourable season, which is now near its termination, and
> more sickness may be expected during the rains; but, from what
> I see, my impression is that, considering its Latitude, the place
> is peculiarly healthy, though the continual heat, especially with
> exposure to the sun or hard labor, will more or less undermine the
> European constitution ... (Barker, 21 Sept 1828).

Barker, like many in the garrison, joined the habit of 'bathing' daily off the beach, despite the presence of saltwater crocodiles. One of the predators had taken one of Smyth's dogs the year before, and when it was spotted again by a sentry, Barker, like all new comers to the north, hurried down to the beach to get his first view of what he called an 'alligator'. The resident crocodile on the beach was nearly 3 metres long and the men made several attempts to catch and kill her*. On 1 November, Barker was:

> … *ready with 3 others with muskets and bayonets to cut off his retreat, but Mills†, always too hot & without judgement, ran at him full butt in the water with a harpoon …*

The crocodile easily evaded him and would not come close again.

A major task for Barker was checking on and increasing the water supply. He had the wells deepened and a new one dug, and personally ventured into the bush to find a fresh water source in the creeks from which the crew of the *Governor Phillip* could fill their barrels, before departing on 22 September. The situation improved greatly, eventually allowing the wells to be more than two metres deep.

A thousand other tasks competed for Barker's attention. Even small things like adding 'a block to the top of the flagstaff, for want of which the flag could not be hoisted high enough & it made us look as if we were in mourning' was important to him (28 October). There was much to learn about his new environment, and his journal is full of descriptions of snakes and lizards, and anything else he found in the bush or the men brought in to him. And there were mysteries to solve: on 4 February, for example, strange lights had been seen in the bush:

> … *A little after 9 pm being doubtful about the lights of last night, combined with the appearance of the Proas today, I went towards the point & again when about half-way, fancied I saw now & then a little brilliant light. I watched sometime without being able to*

---

*   At only 3 metres long and holding a territory, this crocodile was likely to be female.

†   Two men named Mills were at Fort Wellington with Barker: Private James Mills was Barker's servant. The crown prisoner Joseph Mills was a 30-year-old pickpocket who was sentenced for life for the theft of a handkerchief valued at two shillings.

*make out what it was. I then went back for Serjt Drew to point
out the spot where he had seen the light disappear last night &
taking a file of the guard, returned to a part near the point which
he shewed me, & at once discovered the cause of our alarm ... There
was a small swampy place there with high grass, on entering which
numbers of fireflies were disturbed from their resting places on the
stalks & either rose into the air, or emitted their light from time to
time, it being only occasional. This was sometimes so brilliant that I
was not surprised at our seeing it even at the settlement. I was glad
to clear up the mystery ...(Barker, Journal 1829).*

The settlers were also to see some spectacular wildlife sights:

*... The flocks of what we supposed to be birds appeared again
yesterday evening & this evening coming from the opposite side,
but they turn out to be flying foxes. They are so numerous that the
flock is nearly a quarter of an hour passing. Many of them roost
near the back of Peacock's hut ... (8 June 1829).*

Barker started experimenting with local plant foods, collecting
some red apples from trees near the beach* and regularly sending
men out to harvest 'cabbage trees'(the 'hearts' of *Gronophyllum
ramsayi* palms) from the 'cabbage grounds' at the south of the bay,
near the mouth of Sleeman's River. Two types of yams grew near the
settlement, one bitter, one sweet, and Barker sent large parties of men
out to collect them, although he was disappointed that they mostly
found the bitter variety. As shall be seen later in this chapter, Barker
established an excellent relationship with the local Aborigines, and he
was able to seek advice from them about what was edible—something
that, evidently, no one else had thought to do before (Barker, 1829).
Scurvy had finally disappeared, and the health of the population
continued to improve—even the occurrence of fever (probably
malaria) faded under Barker's management (Hartwig, 2007). When
Dr Wilson arrived, there were few health problems at all:

*... On my arrival ... I found every person not only in good
health, but in good condition; and during my residence there, I
observed no complaint amongst the people except ophthalmia ...
(Wilson, 1835).*

---

* *Syzygium suborbiculare.*

As commandant it was Barker's role to keep peace in the settlement, ensure the safety of his people and fair dealings among them, and organise the punishment of any miscreants. The rules were very clear. Each and every person would get an allocation of government food to an exact weight, measured by the commissariat and store keeper. When barrels of salted pork, or peas, for example, were opened for the first time a 'Board of Survey' needed to be convened and the food weighed exactly, and documented, so that there was no opportunity for theft. This usually would involve Barker, the doctor, any other officers available and the commissariat.

Disputes and petty thefts or complaints by the soldiers, the Crown Prisoners or the women, plus the management of spirits, drunken behaviour and all-out brawling took much of Barker's time. Punishment did not always involve flogging (which was rare), locking people in the cells or confining to barracks. More often, in fact, people had their tobacco, or their tea and sugar ration withheld.

On 3 October, Privates John Cook and Haslam had gone foraging in the 'cabbage ground' but Cook did not return. He took a musket and walked off into the forest by himself. In case he was just lost, Barker ordered one of the guns to be fired at intervals to give Cook a direction to find his way back, but by evening he still hadn't returned. Mrs Cook was beside herself and 'very unmanageable from violent grief & lamentations'. She informed Barker that her husband's manner had been very strange for some days—normally a meticulous man, he had given up cleaning his flintlock and declared he was never going to clean it again. When he started talking very strangely to his wife and their child, it was clear he had experienced some sort of breakdown.

Barker sent out search parties, and even went himself on the second day. At one point they found what they thought was Cook's tracks heading south, and they followed them for half an hour before losing them. Barker's search party was a team of eight, and they moved through the country as an extended line, calling out their numbers every few minutes to keep in contact. They followed the run of Sleeman's River for several hours. It was fresh water and Cook must have seen it, so it was not thirst that had been his problem. Numerous tracks of the Iwaidja ran through sections of the bush on this part of the peninsula, and Barker thought it likely that Cook had 'fallen in with them'. On the third day Barker's men were fatigued, so rather than walk, he sent a boat up Sleeman's River to near where Cook's footprints had been seen, to no avail, and the next day they returned to the same area, to climb nearby high ground.

On 8 October, when Cook had been missing for five days, Mrs Cook, desperate in her grief, dressed herself in her husband's clothes and set off alone to find him. Three men had to be sent out to bring her back, and she was then guarded by a sentry. Barker wrote that 'this dressing in men's clothes appears to me to indicate something wild about her'.

On 10 October, Barker took eight soldiers and five Crown Prisoners on a longer search for Cook, carrying three days provisions. They started by whaleboat, then from near Sleeman's River they marched west towards Port Essington and travelled in a big loop back towards the fort. They discovered several good waterholes and learned much useful information about the country, but no sign of Cook was ever found. Poor Mrs Cook was bereft and had nowhere to go. She begged to be allowed to stay in the garrison, rather than sent back to Sydney, and Barker agreed. Of course, this meant she was then the only single woman in camp, and Barker's journal mentions her several times being harassed by men walking past her house, and even calling in. On 9 July:

> ... [Charles] Holt was reported by Mrs Cook to have gone to her hut last night about 11 pm. He denied it but I believe he is guilty. He had gone in there between 8 and 9, when there happened to be Serjt Drew in the hut ... Ordered his Tea, Sugar and Tobacco to be stopped for a month ... (Barker, Journal 1829).

Most of the six women in the garrison were wives of soldiers (a female convict, Mary Rycroft, the wife of crown prisoner

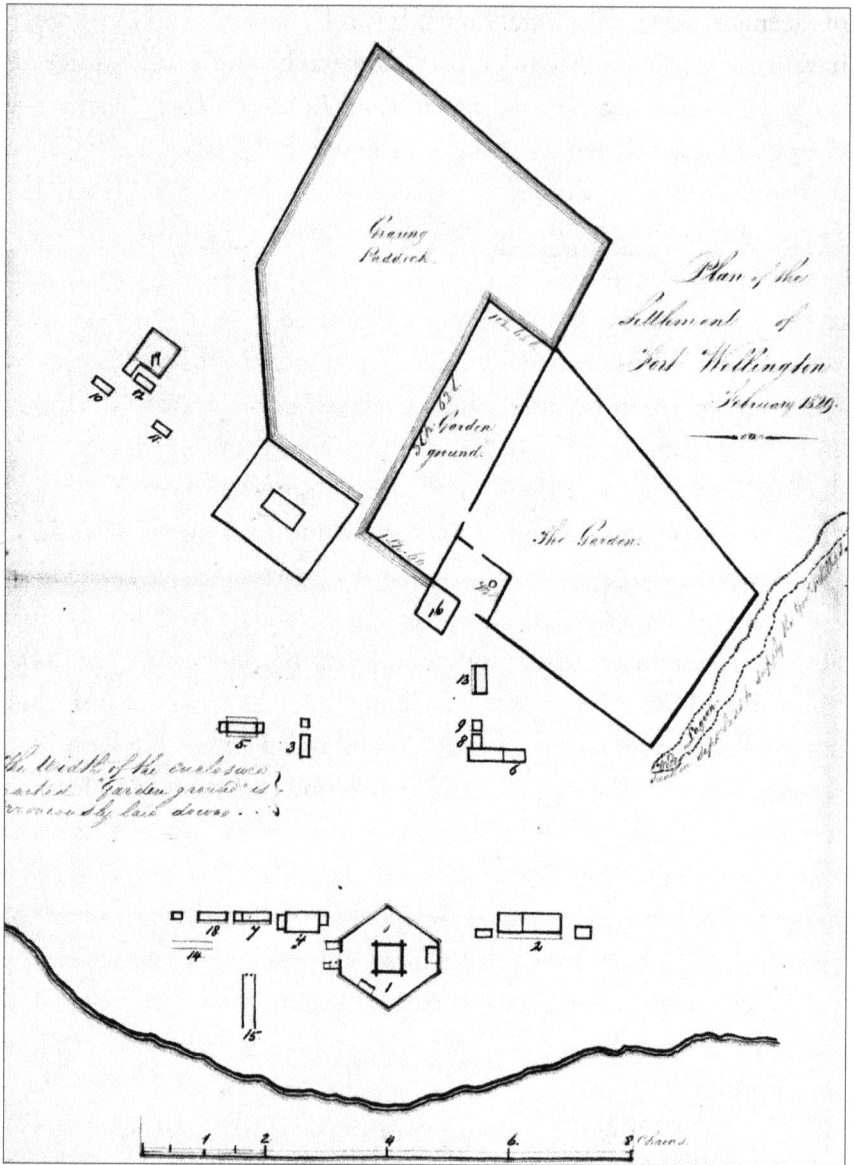

Figure 9: Barker's settlement plan from 1829 (with numbers enhanced)
(NSWSA NRS 906, 4/2060.2).

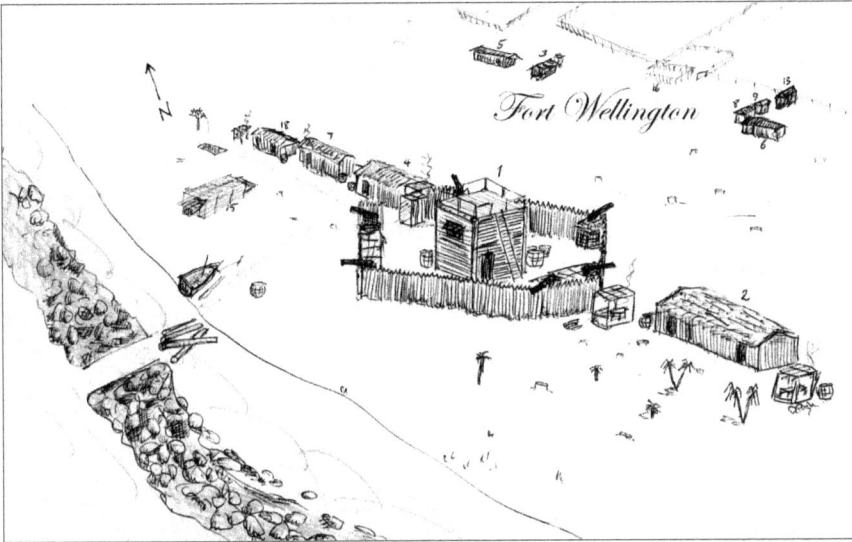

Figure 10: An impression of Fort Wellington based on Barker's map. Sleeman erected a shade roof above the tower to protect the sentries. The roofs were thatched in the first buildings, though bark was also used. A veranda, mentioned by Barker, was also installed on the tower's first floor. Large trees (not shown) must have remained as they were mentioned by d'Urville in 1839.

1 The Fort.	10 Married soldier's hut.
2 Soldiers' barrack.	11 Married soldier's hut.
3 Royal Marines barrack and cookhouse.	12 Small hut.
4 Commissariat.	13 Small hut.
5 Hospital and surgeon's house.	14 Saw pit.
6 Guard house.	15 Boat shed.
7 Crown Prisoners' accommodation.	16 Cattle shed.
8 Married soldier's hut.	17 Pig sties and shed.
9 Married soldier's hut.	18 Crown Prisoners' accommodation.

Table 1: Legend to Barker's 1829 map and the sketch above.

Moxham, came later, when she was transferred from Fort Dundas, on 13 Feb 1829). Apart from Mrs Cook, the other military wives were Mrs Emms, Haslam, Little and Mills, and they all had a role to play. Women were commonly attached to sections of troops in the British army and they did important work. They would cook, clean, wash clothes and mend equipment for each barracks of about 14 men.

One other woman in the settlement was Mrs Oodeen, the wife of the translator and mother of five children.

The Top End climate starts to heat up in October as the season changes. In the 'build up', before the monsoon arrives, the humidity soars, there are few breezes, and the slightest movement can make a person break into sweat. Washing uniforms regularly was essential. On 29 October, Barker allowed the soldiers to remove their belts during the day and just wear their 'kangaroo pouches' because the belts 'excited strong perspiration'. It was so hot at night that Barker himself had been 'forced to get up in the night & walk in the balcony in [his] shirt'. Like every build-up, there was cooling rain and thunder about, but frustratingly, usually only in the distance.

The Crown Prisoners were better off, in terms of climate-suitable clothing, than the military. Each was issued a 'duck frock', a chequered shirt, a pair of duck trousers and a pair of shoes to fit 'as much as possible'. All the men slept in hammocks and they were given blankets, except the marines, who had to supply their own.

Mrs Haslam is mentioned by Barker as suffering a complaint from Private Quinn, who wanted his clothes washed more than once a week. Mrs Haslam refused—'all her other men were satisfied to have their things once a week', and Quinn was told to take his clothes elsewhere.

Unfortunately, the women didn't always get on well with each other, and Barker's patience with them was tried on several occasions. For example, when 'Mrs Emms complained against Mrs Haslam for [a] false report about her and Mr Owen'. Barker thought they were both at fault.

Three of them, Mrs Emms, Haslam and Cook found themselves suffering from fevers in the hospital together, in close confinement for a couple of days, and although they recovered quickly, as time went on the tensions between them rose. In May, Mrs Emms and Mrs Cook were caught brawling, with Mrs Emms 'using very improper language'. Emms put her complaint to the commandant in writing and he decided they were both to blame, but 'Mrs E continued to make a disturbance in spite of my orders to be silent' (Journal 3 May). Without giving us any gossipy details, Barker declared after a hearing, two weeks later, that 'both the women's conduct had been so improper that I should have stopped their rations, had it not been for Mrs Cook's peculiar situation'. Barker may well have regretted his decision to allow Mrs Cook to remain in the community after the loss of her husband.

Two of the Crown Prisoners possessed skills that suggest, in hindsight, that it was only a matter of time before they'd make use of them and make a break. William Henry Hassall and George Neal were sailor navigators—literate men with training in sailing the seas of the world.

In 1813, Hassall had been sentenced to death for his crime of larceny, but the sentence was respited to transportation for life. He arrived in Sydney in February 1814, on the *General Hewitt*. He was then 19 years old, and had survived a rough trip, because thirty-four of his fellow inmates died during the 165-day voyage.

He began working his endless sentence, firstly as a gang worker, then as a servant for a Captain Lethbridge. In 1827, he volunteered for the Raffles Bay settlement and was shipped there on the *Mary Elizabeth*. The following February, he must have eyed the arrival of the Macassan trepang fishermen keenly. Their small ocean-going vessels told him that the East Indies were not that far away.

George Neal had been arrested and tried for 'stealing two shillings worth of goods and chattels', after he and two mates had broken into a house in Bristol. A full jury of twelve found them all guilty and Neal was lucky not to hang. Instead, he was sent to New South Wales in November 1826, for the term of his natural life. His transport was faster than Hassall's, as the *Speke* took just 110 days to arrive in Port Jackson, without losing any of the prisoners on the way. Neal was a sailor through and through, adorned by numerous nautical tattoos; a ship in sail on his chest and a mermaid on his right arm, among them. Still only 21 years old, Neal quickly volunteered to join the Raffles Bay settlement, where he met William Hassall, and the two, with similar backgrounds, became fast friends.

The two men knew how to handle a ship, and must have spent many nights studying the stars, honing their senses of direction. If they could steal a boat, and provision it with water and food, they knew there would then be a good chance of freedom. Clearly, they would need a crew. Who could be trusted to join them?

Other lifers were contenders ... like William Richardson. He had arrived in Port Jackson on 14 February 1827, on the *Albion*. He could read and write, but he was also a carpenter, which was why he'd been recruited for Fort Wellington in the first place. A carpenter's skills would be useful in a small boat.

Another was John Wales, whose crime was breaking and entering, 'burglarously', the house of a widow. Unfortunately for him, he and his older accomplices made too much noise and were apprehended by the widow's servants and watchman. Wales was just 17 and had taken off his shoes to better sneak around the house. His shoes were never returned to him, and he was barefoot at his trial. Ironically, his trade was listed as 'shoemaker'. Wales arrived in Sydney in November 1824 on the *Minerva*. Three years later he was among the volunteer prisoners on the *Mary Elizabeth*, heading for Raffles Bay.

These four, all with life sentences and nothing to lose, hatched a plan to steal the settlement's whaleboat and sail it northwards to freedom. They quizzed Michael McCarthy, the gardener and a fellow lifer who had spent time at Fort Dundas. They needed to know how to avoid Melville Island if they were to escape, and McCarthy knew the passages well. They then collected an axe, and other tools, and at dawn on October 17, 1828, they approached the sentry on duty on the beach. Private Harrison was convinced that they were there legitimately and were to take the whaleboat to go logging a short way up the coast*, rather than the smaller dinghy, because that was broken.

The first Barker knew of the theft was when the convict overseer, Henry Langton, ran up to his room at the fort to report it. Barker immediately ordered Sergeant Shore to take six men and make chase. So, Shore ordered Corporal Parkes and five privates to take the one remaining dinghy and sail and row as fast as they could, after the Crown Prisoners. The drama stretched for hours; as the absconders neared Point Smith the whaleboat was still in sight, but if Barker could see the soldiers drawing close to the larger whaleboat, so too could Hassall and his mates.

> *... I had them pursued in another boat by a party of the Military, who got within half a mile of them without being perceived; they were however much better provided both with Oars and Sails, and, when about Eight miles from the Settlement, our men found it utterly useless to carry on the pursuit ... (Barker, 26 February 1829).*

The escapees locked in the four oars they had stolen and rowed themselves out of range. The soldiers had only two oars, and bad ones at that, so had no chance. Then the weather changed and by mid-morning it was raining, and it continued, sometimes heavily, replete with thunder and lightning, until nearly four in the afternoon. The escapees caught a good breeze and were driven, by it, far out of reach. Hassall, Neal, Richardson and Wales must have been delighted to watch the soldiers drop behind in their dinghy, and then catch the breeze, which

---

* Private Harrison was punished for being deceived: his tobacco and spirits allowance was withheld from him until Christmas day. He lost it again on 5 January for speaking with the prisoners. He claimed he knew William Rushton from Birmingham and they had mutual friends, though Rushton denied this. The outcome was that Barker suspected Harrison was 'half a fool' and was being groomed by several prisoners 'in order to get his assistance to get into the stores'. He therefore reorganised the sentry posts and had Sergeant Shore keep a close eye on Harrison. The same night Private Haslam was found near the stores without reason and was sent to the cells for two days.

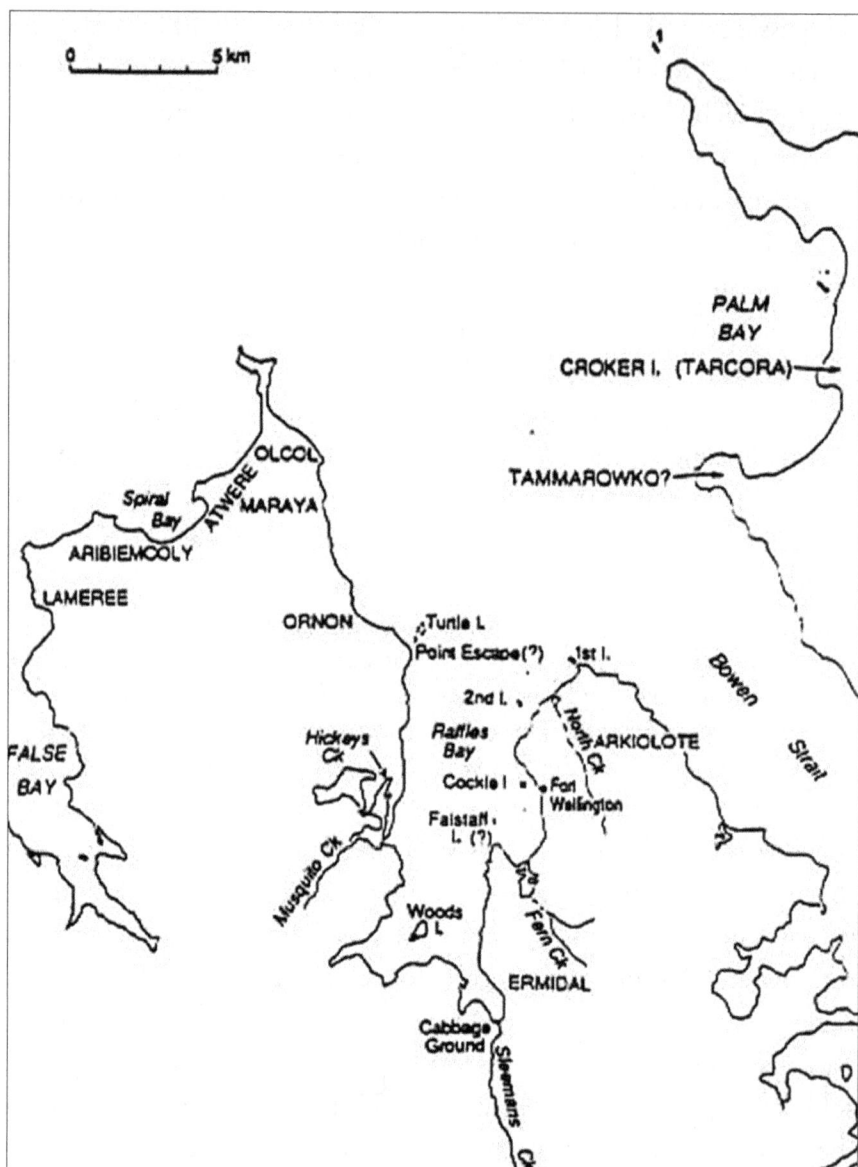

Map 2: Raffles Bay using Barker's place names (Mulvaney, 1993).

whisked them away from their prison shore. We can imagine their joy and sharing whatever the nineteenth century equivalent of 'high fives' must have been. Unfortunately, we'll never know what happened, as none of them were ever heard from again. This either means great success—disappearing is what they wanted and needed to do—or tragic failure, and the latter is what the government hoped for, and they were pronounced dead at sea. This was standard practice, of course, because others needed to be discouraged from trying to escape in the same way, and the threat of death was a useful method of determent.

Barker had his men construct better oars and fitted sails and a new rudder to the small boat, and it was ready by nightfall, but by the next day Barker's ire had dropped, and he wasn't convinced of the boat's seaworthiness. He wrote that he would have taken the boat after the prisoners himself, if there had been another officer in the camp, but he was unwilling to risk the lives of his men. He was more annoyed to find that Hassall had stolen the compass, a barrel (for water?), carpenter's tools and a musket.

Discipline of both the military and the Crown Prisoners was one of Barker's main challenges, and one that he seemed to be particularly adept at, because corporal punishment, in the form of flogging, was needed only four times during his time as Fort Wellington commandant. The Crown Prisoner that suffered the most from the lash was Patrick Devine, an Irish sheep thief on a seven-year sentence, who had gone fishing without permission with three others. As the sun set on 20 October, Devine was tied to a pole and lashed 50 times, by the blacksmith, for 'disobedience of orders, insubordination & disorderly language'. He didn't learn:

> ... On being taken down he said I might get somebody else to work for he would never work in the garden again & used some other expressions of rather a threatening character. On which I sent for a Bible, held a Court on the spot with Dr Davis, & after taking evidence he was sentenced to receive 50 lashes more, twenty five of which I gave him, & then sent him to the hospital ...
> (Barker, Journal 1829).

Two days later Devine was sent back to work, promising 'to keep a better tongue in his head in the future'. Devine's colleagues in the fishing trip, Richards, Craggs and Street, clearly held their tongues better—their punishment was 'to have tea, sugar & tobacco stopt [sic]' (Journal 20 October).

Others who received the lash were Matthew Carr and Joseph Donohoe. Carr was a lifer, convicted of fraud, and seems to have been an impertinent and quick-tempered man, because he was sent to the guardhouse several times, and was involved in fights—chiefly with Devine and Michael Dwyer. Carr stole pumpkins and received 50 lashes on 5 March 1829, and later, at King George's Sound, he continued to get into trouble and was finally sent to Norfolk Island for two years, where he died in 1832.

At the end of December, George Tuesman was sentenced to receive 25 lashes for impertinence, and using a 'most gross expression', in an argument with Langton, the overseer, over who would drink the water used to soak an empty spirit keg overnight. Tuesman apologised sincerely and because the overseer argued on his behalf, he was then let off with a warning. Tuesman had a good reputation, and he was a young man nearing the end of his 7-year sentence. No one objected to this leniency.

Second overseer Joseph Peacock, a 14-year lag who had been court-marshalled for desertion in 1821, was accused of stealing corn belonging to Mrs Emms in October 1828. Barker couldn't find proof, but Peacock appears several times in his journal in regard to corn. In July 1828, Thomas Clark, who worked with Peacock, requested other work, and when questioned, said it was because of Peacock's pilfering and 'making away with the Pig's corn'. Clark was worried about being implicated, as his sentence was nearly up. Barker noted that Peacock's pig was the fattest in the settlement whilst others were fading, and decided to put a watch on Peacock. He set up a system whereby he would be notified when the overseer entered the store, and on 24 July, the call 'Sentry' alerted Barker as Peacock entered the gate of the fort. He then went down and caught him red-handed, with a small bag of corn hidden in his hat. He was sent to the cells, but what disturbed Barker more was Peacock claiming he was providing the corn to Private James Mills, Barker's personal servant. Mills denied involvement emphatically, but Barker was so hurt by the potential disloyalty, he lost sleep. He played chess with Dr Wilson 'wretchedly' that evening because, he wrote, the 'Mills business has quite upset me'.

Mills's house was searched, Mrs Mills questioned, and their stock of corn examined closely, in two days of investigations. Barker eventually concluded that Peacock had been lying and Mills was innocent. All this was happening at the same time John Radford was dying and then his funeral needed to be arranged, and a thousand other things needed Barker's attention.

Peacock was left in the cells for several weeks but was 'closely confined', on 19 August, because he had been found in the Blacksmith's shop during a period of exercise. He survived well enough, nevertheless, and was taken to King George's Sound when Fort Wellington was abandoned. He served out his sentence there, and in Pennant Hills, Sydney, until it expired in 1835.

Missing from the peninsula for several more months were the Aborigines. The Iwaidja kept away from the settlement. They may have had cultural obligations or other reasons to be elsewhere for an extended period, or it may have been just that they were still wary of the British usurpers. After all, several members of their families had been killed and an unknown number had been injured by grapeshot, slugs, or bayonets, during Smyth's time in command.

Commandant Barker continued to impress on his men that times had changed. He told them that, under his regime, the Iwaidja would be treated with 'conciliatory' behaviour. During the search for Private Cook, in the first week of October, Barker felt sure that some of his men would meet Aborigines and he wanted to be sure that any interaction with them would be positive. Dwyer did indeed see one man, in the distance, and found a deserted hut near Sleeman's River, but no other sign of them was found.

A week later Private Little saw a wild dog, whilst on sentry duty, near the hospital, and then five 'very large men' appeared in the bush, but they ran off as soon as Corporal Stagg joined him. The next morning Barker gathered a party together and set off to try and meet them, carrying a knife and some 'hander-kerchiefs [sic] for presents for the blacks' but, despite a three-day search, found no sign of them.

He should have waited at home, because they were visited a few nights later. Private McHugh saw one man, briefly, nosing around their boat, and several were seen on the opposite beach across the bay. Ironically, the boat was under a greater threat than that raised by a nosy Iwaidja tribesman, because it was stolen by Hassell and Neal three nights later, when they made their escape.

In mid-November Barker was walking out near Second Island when he found a spar, which he thought might have been used as a kind of mast for a canoe.

> ... It was hid in the mangroves near the sea & I was first bringing
> it home, but recollecting that they might perhaps have put it there
> for future use, I returned after carrying it some distance & put it
> in the same place ... (Barker, Journal 1829).

This respect for the Iwaidja's belongings marks a turning point. Other British newcomers in the north thought nothing of stealing everything they found, including skulls from graves. Barker was different, but he would have to teach respect, both to his own men and to the Iwaidja. Two nights after he had found the spar, some children's clothing and a barrel was stolen from outside Private Little's house, and barefoot tracks were found aplenty on the paths around the peninsula and on the beach. Barker was frustrated at the lack of a chance to meet with these people, but that chance finally came on 25 November.

Natives were seen during the night, then two were met by Henry Costello, the stockman. They had stuck their spears in the ground, motioned for Costello to approach, then given him a basket. The courage needed from the Iwaidja, for this first friendly encounter in over a year, must have been extraordinary.

Barker and Dr Davis immediately set out to find the two men, taking two handkerchiefs, bread and some scissors as gifts. They soon fell in with a group of ten men, and through rapid, friendly sign language, Barker came to understand they had a white man in their camp, a long way off, and they wanted Barker to accompany them. Perhaps Private Cook was still alive! He promised to join them the next day, and meant it, and he was well aware of the danger when he wrote, that night:

> ... *Closed and settled all the men's accounts for fear of any*
> *accident happening to me tomorrow, as it will not be without risk*
> *that I accompany the natives, but I consider the object justifies*
> *some risk ... (Barker, Journal 1829)*

Unfortunately, there was a storm that evening and the natives didn't come back the next day, or the next few. It was a week until three others were spotted, and this was from a boat. Barker immediately went on shore alone to meet them and one man, who 'seemed to be a chief', met him on the beach. They exchanged presents—Barker gave a handkerchief, and the man gave Barker a spear '& the stick for throwing it'. Barker asked for 'Wellington', the man Smyth had met and nicknamed 18 months earlier. The man pointed to his chest—he was Wellington.

Wellington asked for bread, in English, but it seemed to be the only English word he remembered at the time. Barker had some bread in the boat and sent it up to the Iwaidja before they left. They were both well satisfied with the encounter.

The next week Wellington and Waterloo visited the gardens. At first, they were extremely wary but, mollified by presents, they were reassured by Nonie, one of Oodeen's young daughters, who took Wellington by the hand and then boldly led him into the settlement. Waterloo followed. Barker showed them around, and they visited George Little's pet monkey and the pig sty. Then Barker called for the little girl who was kidnapped from her family nearly a year earlier. She was now known as Mary Waterloo Raffles.

Mary, according to the British, was quite happy to stay with the settlers. She was treated well by Private William Little and his wife, and their son, George. Captain Barker had provided Mrs Little with 'three yards of grey cloth' to make her some dresses. He recorded having a good relationship with the little girl: 'While we were close' he wrote, 'her countenance was sometimes quite animated and her smiles very pleasing.' and he was delighted to report that 'a complete new row of front teeth' had appeared after he was away for a week in Port Essington (Barker, Journal 1829). Bob Innes, in his historical novel about Captain Barker, *Captain of Solitude*, has Barker making friends with Mary by giving her a small plaster doll, complete with a pretty dress and frilly bonnet (Innes, 2019). The fictional exchange highlights the extraordinary change this little Iwaidja girl experienced.

When Wellington and Waterloo visited the gardens, Mary had lived in the settlement for nearly 12 months without meeting any of her people. When at last she did, it was a frightening experience:

> ... *the moment she came she burst into a violent fit of crying, &*
> *turned away her head from them ... I understood Wellington to*
> *point her out as a child of Waterloo. The latter seemed to confirm*
> *it & showed strong though silent emotion*. The water flowed to his*
> *eyes. He lost all his animation, appeared wandering in thought &*
> *trembled violently, which last he continued to do for a long time.*
> *He wanted to take Mary in his arms, but she appeared much*
> *frightened, & when I took her up in mine to calm & soothe her,*
> *the poor little thing put her arms around me & clung to me for*
> *protection ... (Barker, Journal 1829).*

Later, on 17 December, Wellington told Barker that Mary's name was 'Reveral or Reweral' and that she was a 'mandiarawily' (highest class).

Here I need to add a word of caution. The British were happy to identify class divisions among the Iwaidja and felt a need to label Iwaidja people they encountered within a three or four-tiered class system they themselves lived under. The title of 'chief' meant nothing in Iwaidja culture. The 'Social Divisions' described by the British were

---

*   Later Reveral told George that Waterloo was her father but 'it was probably from
     hearing us say so' or that he was one of several men who could be called 'father'
     by her. Another man, named Malmalgah, appeared who was more likely to be her
     actual father.

a misconception of what really was happening. There was never a 'caste system' and the 'classes' which 19th century Englishmen wanted to divide the Iwaidja into, were actually matrilineal moiety divisions, and the way they are described say more about the English system than the Iwaidja:

> ... *The first and highest is named Mandro-gillie, the second,*
> *Manbur-gē, and the third, Mandro-willie ... (Wilson, 1835).*

The categories are still in use today, but modern social organization is more complex, partly because the 'skin' system, which is a relatively recent innovation, is superimposed on the older system of semi-moieties (Birch, 2014). With this in mind, we need to take words like 'mandiarawily' and 'chief' when they appear in the journals with a grain of salt. Some of the 19th century commentary on Iwaidja culture is appended for interest's sake.

In the meantime, back in November 1828, two other men, Mago and Nonie (the same name as Oodeen's child), came into the settlement, and received presents. Barker tried to get information about Cook, but communication was very difficult, and Reveral would not help. When they left, Barker 'half-fancied as they were going off that they made signs that they would bring a white man with them', but nothing was ever found of Cook, so it was probably just fancy. His hospitality tempered by realism, Barker was pleased to see all the Aborigines were terrified of the garrison's dogs, as they were the best guards at night.

The next time Barker saw Waterloo and Mago, they had just been given a shave and a hair cut by some of the soldiers, and he didn't recognise them at first. He noticed that the two had scars on their bodies and when asked about them, signed that they had come from wounds received by the attack on them a year before by Smyth's men. Their nervousness about coming into the settlement was highly justified.

On 11 December, Barker accompanied Wellington, Waterloo and Mago into the bush. Barker went unarmed, which gave the Iwaidja great confidence. They invited him to Croker Island with them, but, as it was so far, Barker had to decline at that time.

The next week, Wellington brought his son to meet Barker, a 'fine lad of about 18 of more intelligence & animation than the others', and he and Waterloo were given hatchets and fish-hooks, but this led to a surprising level of antagonism from Wellington, who was 'seeming to think that he as chief was undervalued'. Barker then felt he had to give Wellington another hatchet to keep him happy. Wellington's:

> ... power as chief may have spoilt his temper. He seems to be
> selfish & jealous [when] his companions, particularly Waterloo,
> are paid more attention than himself ... (Barker, Journal 1829).

Just before Christmas, Barker decided to try and capture a turtle for the men for their Christmas dinner, so he gathered a party and they rowed the 12 miles to Turtle Island and camped overnight in tents. There were no turtles that night, but in the morning they were joined by Waterloo and three strangers who came across the bay in a canoe to see them. The Iwaidja were very impressed by the tents and helped the soldiers hunt for turtles, although they too, were unsuccessful this time. It was then they participated in a very un-British group act which astonished the white men:

> ... After going a little way they stopped & seemed to be asking us
> to do something we could not understand. Waterloo & the chief
> then stooped down in an attitude not to be mistaken, motioning
> us to do the same. Their example was soon followed by the two
> others, & each scooping a little hole on the sand with his hand
> obeyed the calls of nature or custom with great sang froid, talking
> at the same time to his companions. Then they covered up the
> place and got up nearly together ... (Barker, Journal 1829).

That afternoon Barker also met Wellington and he was again invited to join the Iwaidja in their camp, but he again had to refuse because it was too close to Christmas Day and he had duties in the settlement.

Christmas was as traditional as they could make it. Everyone was issued extra flour, raisins and suet for plum puddings, and alcohol flowed freely enough to land Privates Leary, Higgins and Duffield in the guard house for riotous behaviour. Sergeant Harvey complained that Private Walsh had struck him, so Walsh was arrested. He was, perhaps, a man no one wanted to be hit by—the settlement didn't have any handcuffs big enough to fit his ham fists.

Boxing Day was spent tracking down the source of the alcohol (Haslam's House), pack drilling the miscreants as punishment and, in the evening, hosting Mago and two strangers, Alobo and Nagary. The Iwaidja demonstrated their skills in spear throwing and singing into the evening. Langton was detailed to look after them, and he pitched a tent on the beach for them to stay the night. In the morning Barker had a cannon fired, which awed and frightened them, and they were keener to watch the sawyers cut a tree in half. They parted good friends: the Iwaidja promising to return, and Barker promising to visit them on Croker Island.

Over the turn of the year, the settlement may have had a near-miss from a cyclone. The weather was so bad, gale force winds knocked trees down around them. In hindsight it could have been a forewarning for Victoria Settlement in Port Essington. Ten years later, Victoria was destroyed, lives were lost, and the *Pelorus* driven ashore, by a cyclone.

In Raffles Bay the storm seemed to have brought sickness. Both Wellington and Waterloo were struck down with fevers, headaches and sore throats and Barker ended up sailing them across to Croker Island, to deliver them to the care of family members. It was a huge favour, as the British then had to row 12 miles back to the fort against the wind. Barker was beginning to tire of Wellington's begging system: 'in a style that gave me a very unfavourable opinion of him after the kindness that we had shewn him'. He reported to MacLeay that:

> ... *Another of our difficulties with them arises from their great Character of Chief being a man of bad temper, and professing an insatiable desire for presents, so that it requires much address to keep him in good humour without giving way to him* ... *(Barker, 26 February 1829).*

Barker also recorded his feelings in his journal:

> ... *Wellington certainly is of a sulky dissatisfied temper & I fear*
> *there will be some difficulty keeping on good terms with him*
> *without humouring him, which I do not consider should be done*
> *to any great degree. But we must not expect perfection in such*
> *a race & I shall endeavour to keep on friendly terms & make*
> *allowances, as far as can be done without appearing to bend to*
> *them ... (Barker, Journal 1829).*

Wellington recovered his health and his good humour returned. He seemed contrite and subdued when Barker quizzed him about his poor behaviour a few days early—he had demanded a hatchet from Private Leary and threatened to hit him with hoop iron when Leary refused to give it to him.

For a few nights in mid-January, larger numbers of men started to sleep overnight in the tent, until Barker protested that he could not feed so many. Most returned to their own camps, although Wellington and two others, Marinbel and Lugo, slept again in the tent. Wellington that night told Barker that, as he was chief of all, Barker should not be giving presents to anyone, except through him.

On 29 January, Mago, Alobo and Waterloo visited the settlement and the tent was pitched for them on the beach as usual. Waterloo was ill at the time, but Mago and Alobo were in fine form, entertaining the British by singing and dancing. Mago had brought along an instrument which was, until then, unrecorded by the British:

> ... *a large hollow cane about 3 feet long bent at one end.*
> *From this he produced two or three low and tolerably clear &*
> *loud notes, answering to the tune of didoggery whoan, & he*
> *accompanied Alobo with this while he sang his treble ...*

The Iwaidja word for didgeridoo is *ardawirr*, but Barker's description of its sound; '*didoggery whoan*', demonstrates the onomatopoeic origins of the word 'didgeridoo'.

The British tried to join in, with a clumsy attempt at rhythm:

> ... *The Dr & some others were beating time with their hands*
> *during the first song, & when the second was going to begin,*

*Mago begged they would not add their accompaniment, which it
must be confessed was not an improvement ...*

Mago and Alobo then spent that afternoon being shaved by
Thomas Potts and played with the children 'for a considerable time'.
Mago:

*... Piled all their hats on his head, & endeavouring by sitting on
a high stump to prevent them being able to knock off & playing
other children's tricks with them ...*

Relationships with the Iwaidja continued to flourish. In
February:

*... This evening the whole of the natives were in great glee
dancing in front of the marines' huts. They thought to astonish us
by some feats of activity & imitations of animals in their dance
but were in turn astonished by one of the Crown Prisns, who had
been a tumbler (Potts), being brought to exhibit some of his feats,
dancing & walking on his hands & other mountebank's tricks
which they found beyond their ability ... They continued to sing
until 8¹/² pm, I being obliged to feed them as usual, when they all
lay down in the tent ...*

Despite this friendliness, the Iwaidja lived a culture as foreign to
the British as was possible. Theirs was a complex world of traditional law,
kinship responsibilities, art and ceremony, whilst the British relied on a
class system and made decisions based on the desires of their monarch
on the other side of the world. The British caught tiny glimpses of the
Iwaidja culture as they listened to songs they couldn't understand and
clapped along to dances whose meaning was lost. Curious Aborigines
all along the coast had had contact with outsiders for decades and
knew that the newcomers had technologies which would be useful to
them, knew that most came solely to take things away, like trepang and
hawksbill turtles, and that foreigners were often dangerous. The trust
that Barker had been able to develop between the settlement and the
Iwaidja was something new in that part of the coast. The Macassans
talked about 'good' Aborigines further east along the coast (Barker,
Journal 1829), who treated them well, and were sometimes employed
by them, and even occasionally journeyed to Macassar with them in

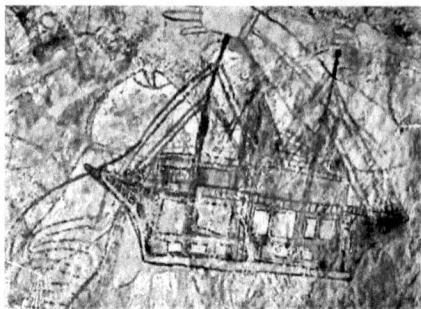

Figure 11: Tall ship painting at Djulirri, Wellington Ranges.

the off-season (MacKnight, 2017). These groups would trade with Aboriginal groups for turtle shell, ironwood and pearl shells, in return for food, tobacco, alcohol, cloth, and axes. The Iwaidja were much less trusting, and may not previously have been the recipients of this trade, relying on theft for items such as canoes instead.

Some 30 kilometres from the Arnhem coast (south of Goulburn Island) there is a sandstone massif called The Wellington Range. It was never visited by the British settlers, but numerous rock overhangs and cliffs there have provided shelter for Australians for thousands of years. On their walls people have painted in ochres and clays and produced some of the most outstanding rock art galleries found anywhere. At a site called *Djulirri* there is a series of historical 'contact' paintings that reveal relationships between local Aboriginal groups and visitors to their shores (Taçon & May, 2013). The 1100 paintings at Djulirri include images of Macassan praus and *keris* knives, brigs and steam ships, and white men standing with their hands on their hips (or in their pockets), horses and guns.

One of the ship paintings looks like a two masted brig such as the *Amity*, or the *Governor Phillip*. It would be wonderful to be able to emphatically identify its subject and trace its connection to Fort Wellington, but this is not possible (May, et al., 2013). The painting has been retouched many times and may in fact represent any, or all, of the ships the artist was familiar with. One study dated the oldest parts of this painting to the 1700s, which means it might have been a Dutch ship, rather than British (Taçon, et al., 2010). The painting remains an attractive connection between the Aborigines and the early visitors of the eighteenth and nineteenth centuries.

By February 1829, Barker had good reason to be pleased with the way things were going:

> ... we are at present on very good terms with the Natives, who frequently come into the Settlement, sleep in a Tent which I pitch for them, and whose friendship seems likely to continue. Our first intercourse was on the 25th November last, and was attended with much fear and suspicion on their part; one means of dispelling which has been the kindness with which they have seen the Native Girl treated. They are not all that I could wish for, but we must make allowances for an uncivilized race; and I have treated them with great indulgence, where I could do so, without leading them to suppose I courted their friendship through fear ... (Barker, 26 February 1829).

The settlement grew twice in 1829: on 14 February and 15 April, when the *Amity*, under its newly appointed commander, William Owen, and the *Lucy Ann*, under Captain Powditch, arrived with people and stock from Fort Dundas. The people included 13 Crown Prisoners, one of whom was a woman (Mary Ann Rycroft), and seven members of the 57th Regiment of Foot, who would be staying in the settlement. Captain Hartley was with them and was relieved to be sailing south to Sydney on the *Lucy Ann*, but the *Amity* was now to be permanently stationed in Raffles Bay to undertake supply trips to Timor.

The stock from Melville Island included sheep, goats, and pigs, one of which was a boar that caused too much trouble over the next few days, by breaking into the gardens, because there was nowhere strong enough to hold him. It was slaughtered, but its dark meat was unfit to eat and so it was boiled up to feed the other pigs and dogs (Barker, Journal 1829).

Unloading the *Lucy Ann* took several days. The supervision of the stores was mainly done by Mr Hickey, the storeman, and John Radford, the Deputy Assistant Commissary General (DACG) from Fort Dundas, who was also to now be stationed in Fort Wellington, along with his servant, Joseph Donohoe.

The *Lucy Ann* departed on 27 February, leaving behind a small schooner for use in Raffles Bay. It was worm-ridden and rotten, needed caulking and cleaning, a new boom and other renovations before she was useful, but after about a week's work filling worm holes, she proved 'tolerably water-tight'. Barker now had a vessel suitable for exploring Port Essington, and though he was delayed by bad weather for days, he took a week-long expedition there in March, during which he mapped the port and searched for water sources. Unfortunately, the maps, which he refers to many times in his journal, have been lost, although they may have been well-used ten years later when Sir Gordon Bremer brought a party of new settlers into the bay, to establish Victoria Settlement.

About that time the *Amity* was sent to Timor for supplies, with John Radford aboard to do the shopping, 'he being indeed the only person on this establishment capable of performing this duty with advantage to the public service' (Hartley, 1829). Other sails were soon spotted on the horizon at that time too, the first of the Macassan trepang fleet arrived in the bay on March 23.

As soon as the praus were seen, Barker sent the Doctor and Oodeen out to greet them and invite them into the settlement. They were at first wary but needed water, and they eventually agreed. One of the captains was Narrein, the brother of Deing Riolo, who was not coming that year because he had wrecked his prau on the way home, in 1828. Barker offered the Malays protection and friendship and quizzed them about their industry: seventy praus had left Macassar two or three months before, but they had little success in catching trepang up to that time, and most of them were therefore heading to Port Essington to try their luck there. Narrein, with black teeth and red, betel nut stained lips, could not read a map, but he knew his way around the north coast well. He said that Raffles Bay was a healthy place, but they usually had trouble with the natives there. He, and the other prau captains who came, were thrilled there was now a British settlement in the bay, and though they had nothing to trade in the 1829 season, they promised that when they returned in 1830, they would bring many items.

Major Campbell summarised what he knew of the Malays in 1834:

> ... *The name given to this coast and its native inhabitants by the Malays is ' Marega.' They call Port Essington 'Limboo Moutiara' (Port of Pearl-shell); and the Aborigines call the Malays 'Mulwadies' The Malays represent that they found the natives extremely troublesome and hostile all along the northern coast; and they were glad when in Raffles Bay, at the time of our having a settlement there, they found themselves protected from the Indians, and were able to repair their vessels without being molested by them. Previous to our occupation of Raffles Bay they were accustomed to resort for these purposes to a small island outside, close to the west point of entrance into the bay ... (Campbell, 1834).*

Deing Riolo's uncle arrived on 1 April. He had been visiting the trepang grounds for 40 years, sometimes travelling as far as the Gulf of Carpentaria, and he was happy to talk of the economics of the industry. He complained that there were now too many boats fishing, and most would go back only half full.

The next day, a small prau, under Captain Pamoomoo, came in for shelter and food, because they had lost their rice to the natives somewhere. He requested permission from Barker to set out with a retribution party into the bush to punish Aborigines, which of course, Barker refused, even though:

> *He & his people described them (the Aborigines) as very bad, said they eat men & had eaten a Malay last year (Barker, Journal 1829).*

One of the captains told Barker, in May, that the natives on the west coast of Arnheim [sic] Bay, had taken a prau and killed the captain and most of the crew. Only four sailors had escaped and one of them was pointed out to Barker. There may have been skirmishes all along the coast for years to the detriment of both sides: in February an Iwaidja man named Eaboork had described how several of his people had been shot by the trepangers.

During the 1829 season, Barker recorded 1053 Malay visitors on 36 praus, ranging in size from those with a crew of 17, to those with 49 crewmen. All of them had behaved well, without a single instance of drunkenness, which impressed Barker, as alcohol was a constant source of problems among his own men.

On 6 April, a stranger staggered into the settlement just after dawn, with two spear wounds in his legs. De'Atea was a Malay fisherman, and he claimed he had been shipwrecked several months before. He and two companions had managed to get to shore by canoe, somewhere in Port Essington, where they'd been met by natives who 'ill-treated' them. De'Atea escaped and knew nothing more of his companions. Searches were undertaken for the two missing Malays, and the Iwaidja questioned closely, but they denied any knowledge of the men.

Four natives visited the beach near the settlement that night but did not come in. The soldiers were 'excited against them by the treatment of the shipwrecked Malays'. Then a report came in that Matthew Carr had been 'carried off by the blacks'. After setting off in alarm with the guard, Barker found Carr was safe, but had been hassled by Mago and two others until he had run away. Barker sent six soldiers out to look for, and apprehend Mago, so that he could express his displeasure.

De'Atea recovered quickly from his wounds and when two natives, Yangun and Mayawen, entered the settlement on 13 April, De'Atea immediately recognised them. He said Mayawen was present when he'd been speared. Barker felt sure that they could therefore find the two missing Malays, if they chose to help, but did not trust them without some sort of leverage. Barker then made one of his few mistakes in cross-cultural relationships at the settlement, made even worse when he discovered it was all based on a lie: he held Yungun hostage and sent Mayawen off to find the ship-wrecked Malays.

The Iwaidja were shocked. Waterloo, Alobo, Nagary and another man soon arrived near the settlement, nervous that they were about to be shot at, or detained themselves. Barker went out to see them:

> … *They all asked anxiously for Yungun & appeared wanting to know why he was kept. I again attempted to explain that they must go look after the Malays, & when they were brought to the settlement Yungun would be released & they rewarded … (Barker, Journal 1829).*

Barker then took Yungun in the schooner with him on a search of the coast for the Malays. The day passed quickly, so they camped at Relief Point and continued searching the next morning. It was 15 April, and the *Amity* arrived, bringing the very last of the stores, cattle, troops and Crown Prisoners from Melville Island. Barker was now torn between his duty to the settlement and his search for the Malays. He decided to land Yungun on the east point of False Bay (now Bremer Bay) and return to Raffles Bay. To add to the confusion, it was just a few days before Easter, and dozens of praus were now arriving, mustering together before their fleet returned to Macassar, together.

One of the Macassan captains, Damatian, offered to take De'Atea back to Macassar, but he was 'determinedly anxious to remain' and Barker allowed him, as he would be a useful worker in the gardens. Then, on 8 May, a Macassan captain and his crew visited, planning to bury one of their own on the beach near the settlement. De'Atea immediately hid himself in the overseer's room, and when, later, he was questioned, the true story came out. He was, in fact, a runaway slave from a prau named *Tanalati*, under Captain Yaicha, and he hadn't been shipwrecked at all. He had been speared whilst resisting some Aborigines who wanted his clothing, and the two Malays whom Barker searched for, and kidnapped Yungun as a hostage for, never existed. De'Atea's lies had wasted a lot of Barker's time, but he was lucky: Barker believed that a runaway slave, having reached British soil, had gained his freedom, so, however distasteful doing so was to him, he extended De'Atea British protection, and would not give him up to the Macassan captain.

De'Atea certainly pulled his weight afterwards. He worked daily in the gardens, and remained in the settlement until it closed. He was then dropped off in Timor:

> ... De'Atea was left in charge of Mr. Tielmann, who promised to take care of him until he found a better situation ... This poor fellow, who was much esteemed on account of his good humour and obliging disposition, usually worked in the garden at Raffles Bay, where he performed more labour than two or three convicts, who being sent from home, according to their own account, for doing nothing, adhere to their favourite propensity of doing as little as possible elsewhere ... We found that De'Atea understood very imperfectly the Malayese, as spoken at Koepang, which, it appears, differs considerably from the Celebese dialect. He regretted being left at Koepang; and, had his own wishes been acceded to, he would willingly have accompanied Captain Barker, at parting with whom he was exceedingly distressed, following the boat till nearly up to his neck in water, embracing the Captain's knees, and weeping bitterly ... (Wilson, 1835).

In the beginning of March, Wellington and a small group of Iwaidja were in the settlement, and one of them stole a knife. A man named Macoa was found with it. Barker arrested him and was planning to flog him as punishment, until Wellington convinced him that Macoa was innocent, and the real thief had 'made off at the first alarm'. Only Wellington, Marinbel and Luga stayed that night, but they left the next morning 'rather dissatisfied' and were not seen again for nearly two months, when Wellington and Luga reappeared on the opposite shore of the bay, wanting to prove their friendship with presents of spears and baskets.

Relationships with the Iwaidja soured after Yungun's kidnapping and the knife theft. Waterloo apparently stole a puppy from Joseph Peacock, the second overseer, whilst conversely, Mago was loaned a dog for a couple of days, but brought it back as agreed, despite the women crying when it was taken away.

On 2 June, a canoe went missing during the night, probably taken by Lugo and three others. Barker took a party up the coast and they retrieved it but couldn't positively identify the thieves. Another canoe was stolen on 11 June, and they only got it back when the thieves ran off after Private Neale brought his musket up.

However, nearly every day some of the Iwaidja would visit the settlement as friends, despite the increasing nocturnal mischief. Some even laboured in the fields for the community, delighting in the use of tools.

On the night of 17 June, Yungun broke into the cookhouse and later cut off a section of a seine net left in front of the barracks, but he was spotted and dropped it as he fled into the sea, swimming around the coast.

Then, on 22 June, Lugo came into the settlement with 6 others:

> ... I immediately ordered him to be seized, & had him put into one of the cells, in the hope that by punishing him I might put a stop to their night depredations, showing him that we were able to discover the perpetrators. He, as well as the others, was much alarmed ... Waterloo was in much fear, especially when I made him understand I suspected him to be one of the canoe stealers. ...

The others were assured that they were welcome to stay, and they ate fish and rice, and slept on the ground between the guard house and the fort. The next day, two of them, Rojaro and Nagary, left early whilst the others

> ... begged very hard for Lugo ... Having determined, however, to give him a few lashes, I had him taken handcuffed to the waterside. To impress on them the more that I made a distinction between good & bad conduct, I had previously given Momomeyon a tomahawk ... making him understand that it was because he had always behaved well, but that I intended to punish Luga, as I should anyone whom I discovered coming by night to steal from us ... When my motives were thoroughly understood, I made him (Luga) receive about twenty lashes... (Barker, Journal 1829).

Lugo was put back in the cells to wait for the excitement to die down. Barker wanted his companions to beg for his release again so it would look like he was doing them a favour. When he was freed an hour or two later, everyone was happy.

But, in the early afternoon the alarm was raised. Rojaro and Nagary had gone to get help, and a party of about 40 men were gathering at the edge of the settlement, expecting a fight. They relaxed when they found that Lugo had been freed, and Barker was taken to meet their leaders, old men named Oologheny and Wadyere. It was clear to Barker that most of these men had crossed from Croker Island specifically on Lugo's behalf, but he was never sure if their intentions had really been hostile or not. He fed the chiefs and gave them presents, and most went home that afternoon.

Just two days later another attempt was made to steal a canoe. Barker suspected Waterloo and two others, but the canoe was recovered when the alarm went up.

Wellington and Marinbel visited on 25 June and Barker offered to go with them and stay overnight with their people. Together they walked several kilometres to a clearing in the forest that had a white sand floor, no sand flies and 'very few Musquitos'. It was a friendly outing, Barker even discovered Wellington's real name was Merriak. Barker was very relaxed:

> … A fire was made instantly & the manner of my two
> companions had been so free from suspicion that I lay down in
> perfect confidence & slept very soundly …

They returned to the settlement for a night and Wellington slept in the overseer's house. The next day Barker went with Wellington and Marinbel to meet their families because they were not far away. Barker's journal entry for 27 June is as long as it was potentially momentous, for up until then, none of the British had met any Iwaidja women or children:

> … I determined to go & pass the night with them, & thus try the
> experiment of what perfect confidence may do in making their chief
> friendly, who may perhaps be useful in preventing the depredations
> of some of the others … We proceeded at a brisk walk towards
> Olcol when they expected to find their people … On coming

*to a part called Ornon we found traces ... & here I discovered
what I previously thought probable, that they were almost as well
acquainted with the foot marks of their friends as we are with the
countenances of ours. Wellington severally shewed them to me ... &
seemed to have great delight in pointing out those of his wife & one
or two of his children ... (Barker, Journal 1829).*

They moved off after the tracks and on the way the Iwaidja
showed Barker how to find bush honey, spear fish in a river, and
then light a fire using a dry stick. They cooked and ate at a place
called 'Aribiemoolly', where Wellington had expected their families
to be. They moved on to a larger camping area near False Bay, and
Wellington pointed out who slept where, but the camp was deserted,
and they were disappointed not to meet anyone. The next day, whilst
travelling back towards the settlement, they came across Luga and
four boys, three of which were Wellington's sons and one Luga's. The
women had hidden in the bush and nothing would get them to come
out. In fact, only one woman was ever seen by members of the Fort
Wellington garrison, and she had been bayoneted and her baby shot,
on the night Reveral was kidnapped. The fear the women had of the
Englishmen may have stemmed from this event.

Barker's journal entry about this excursion is long and full of
detail, which must have taken him hours to write and, as his days
were so busy, he probably sat up late into the night to finish it.

John Radford was a trusted public servant who performed well
at Melville Island. During the first few months of 1829, Radford
was sent to Timor on several supply runs on the *Amity*, but things
seemed to start to unravel for him during the year. He was a heavy
drinker, and on 19 April, Barkly reported a 'disturbance at the
cottage' where Radford lived. He sent Dr Davis to sort it out, but
it was too late: Radford and his friend Lieutenant Owen (of the
Amity) and others, had been drinking wine most of the day. There
was then:

*... an affray between Mr. Owen ... and Private Little 39th Regt
and from Mr Radford's servant Durham [Donohoe] being very*

> *riotous and wanting to fight also. The latter Sergeant Shore had*
> *put in the Guardhouse. I ordered Little there also and two others*
> *of the 39th. Mac, Hugh and Clay, who I understood were drunk,*
> *but Little requesting to be brought before me, I saw that he was*
> *perfectly sober and finding he had received great provocation*
> *released him ... (Barker, Journal 1829).*

The 'great provocation' involved Mrs Little, and a couple of other soldiers' wives, partying in the cottage with the gentlemen. Little had stood outside the cottage calling his wife, to no avail, and Mr Hickey, the storekeeper, had encouraged him to go inside and collect her. Someone then clubbed Little over the head with a candlestick, cutting him badly. Donohoe was blamed and taken to trial. Radford was affronted, because he refused to acknowledge that the commandant had any authority over his assigned servant, but, nevertheless, on 20 April, Barker:

> *... held a bench for the trial of Crown Prisoner Dunham [sic], Mr*
> *Radford's servant. Parade at 5.30 PM when Dunham received 50*
> *lashes pursuant to sentence ... (Barker, Journal 1829).*

Donohoe's lashes were landed for the crime of being 'turbulent and disorderly' after a 'riot at the cottage', and for missing church parade. Barker and Dr Davis then spent time investigating the riot, which led to both Radford and Owen apologising. Radford promised that it would never happen again, and Owen was ready to 'make any consideration for the man'. However, it was Donohoe who had borne the brunt of the punishment.

The affray was forgotten during May, when the *Amity* was once again sent to Timor for supplies. She returned in the afternoon of 30 June, bringing sheep, buffaloes, fruit trees, and the fresh food John Radford had bought in Kupang, plus some strangers: five sailors from the shipwrecked *Governor Ready* were working their passage back to Sydney, plus a Royal Navy Surgeon, named Dr Wilson. The latter vastly improved Barker's social life over the next few months. He was Barker's social equal, and a man whose 'ideas on the subject of the natives coincide(d)' with Barker's. Wilson agreed, for example, that 'most of the quarrels with the blacks have commenced with a fault on our side'.

All convict transport ships had a doctor on board to care for the health of the convicts, their guards and their crew. Crown Prisoners weren't always healthy, and the doctor had the right to unload them, before they departed Great Britain, if he thought there was a chance that they would die on the way to the colonies. In 1828, the *Governor Ready*, under Captain Young, was chartered to carry 190 male convicts from Ireland to New South Wales. The doctor on board was 'Surgeon-Superintendent' Thomas Braidwood Wilson, a Scot who had trained in Edinburgh. There was a crew of 48, and 50 privates of the 63rd Regiment stood guard over the convicts. Captain Young and Dr Wilson had already made one trip together, taking 190 convicts to Van Diemen's Land, and had returned, via Isle de France, with a cargo of sugar which was mostly spoiled by salt water during a storm, losing the investors a lot of money. With a damaged reputation, Captain Young found there was no one offering a backload of freight from Sydney, so he decided to return to England via Batavia, and seek a cargo there.

Figure 12: Surgeon Thomas Braidwood Wilson.

Wilson wasn't impressed. He had previously suffered the diseases and discomfort of Batavia and would have preferred to avoid returning there. In the end, he never did, because the *Governor Ready* hit an outcrop of coral in the Torres Strait so fast, that it was immediately clear she was wrecked and without hope. The 39 officers and crew luckily had enough time to unload the longboat, a skiff, and a jolly boat, and collect food, water, and other supplies from the ruined ship. They also found water on nearby islands before setting off on a 1300-kilometre journey towards Melville Island, hoping to reach the settlement at Fort Dundas. It was 10 May 1829. They would eventually travel 1800 kilometres and arrive in Koepang, Timor, on 2 June 1829.

Wilson saved his journal from the wreck, and spent the long days in the long boat keeping it up to date. He published it in *A*

Narrative of a Voyage Round the World, in 1835, and it makes for excellent reading, even with consideration of his nineteenth century writing style and enthusiastic hyperbole (for instance, water found on Half Way Island was an 'inestimable fluid' and when the crew found a 'reservoir' in the rocks, they were able to indulge 'in copious and unrestrained potations') (Wilson, 1835).

The boats were hit by a gale near Melville Island and it was impossible to steer them into Aspley Strait to reach Fort Dundas, so they stayed with the wind and arrived in Port Concordia, in Koepang, Timor, a few days later. It was fortunate, because Fort Dundas had already been abandoned, and the outcome of their trip might have been very different if they had managed to get there.

Wilson delights in telling his readers about Koepang (Kupang), the hospitality they enjoyed, and especially about a fortuitous meeting with an old friend ...

John Radford, the deputy assistant commissary general at Fort Wellington, had arrived on the *Amity*, and was busy buying supplies for the fort. The two had a tearful reunion when Radford recognised Wilson among a heavily bearded, motley group of shipwrecked sailors.

Wilson had no desire to return to Batavia, where Captain Young and most of the rest of the crew were headed, for fear of disease. Rather, he was excited to be invited to join Radford, and take the opportunity to explore the north of New Holland, and Raffles Bay, whilst waiting for a ship back to Sydney. So, when the *Amity* sailed, on 8 June, Dr Wilson and five of his companions, one of whom was a carpenter, were also on board.

Radford loaded the ship with 19 buffaloes, 10 sheep, maize and as much fruit and vegetables as he could purchase, and they departed for Raffles Bay on 8 June 1829. It was a stressful journey. Lieutenant Owen struggled to keep the *Amity* afloat. She was becoming ever more unseaworthy and leaking badly. Soon after departure, Owen decided to go back to Koepang to repair a leak, and once they had got back under way, the ship had to beat against contrary currents, and a 'monsoon', and skirt large areas of previously uncharted reefs, which Wilson named Owen's or Barker's Reefs.

The merchant contact in Timor was Monsieur Becharde, who had supplied the Fort Dundas settlers for several years. Becharde was frustrated at the lack of skilled workers in Koepang and the services available. So much so, in fact, that he sent a coffee-mill to Fort Wellington on the *Amity* to be repaired by a mechanic there. If nothing else, this demonstrated confidence in the new settlement.

So too, did the increasing health and happiness of the community. There was now time for recreation and what was, perhaps, the first game of 'football' to be played in north Australia, occurred on the beach on 24 July 1829:

> *... Our men this morning having got a bladder from a Buffalo that was killed had a fine game of football for half an hour & seemed to enjoy it. Football at Raffles Bay, Latitude 11° 13'!!! ... (Barker, Journal 1829).*

The *Amity* arrived, still badly leaking, in Raffles Bay on the '31st of June' 1829 [sic] (Wilson, 1835). Dr Wilson was immediately introduced to the commandant and was well received. Collet Barker, as commandant, had been starved of the company of gentlemen during his time at the fort, so when a fellow well-educated man of a similar background arrived, he must have been thrilled. They became good friends, and their relationship shines through Wilson's narrative, and it is much better for it. They played chess together, Barker concluding that 'a cool attack of [Wilson's] occasional mistakes could either beat him or change his system' (Barker, Journal 1829).

Wilson recognised some of the prisoners and guards of the 63rd Regiment who had been transported with him on the *Governor Ready*, although he did not name them, and he was impressed with the little settlement and the health of its occupants:

> *... On my arrival ... I found every person not only in good health, but in good condition; and during my residence there, I observed no complaint amongst the people except ophthalmia ... (Wilson, 1835).*

Dr Wilson moved into Radford's house, the shingled cottage on the hill, as a guest of his friend, and was thus in a good position to notice changes in him when he started to complain of pain and illness, almost from the moment he returned from Koepang. Within two weeks he was confined to bed, unable to move for the pain. Dr Davis cared for him 'sedulously', but the disease was identified by Wilson as 'acute hepatitis ... supervening on the chronic form'.

Radford died on 24 July, just before midnight. A 'quart of matter proceeded from [his] liver ... it seemed wonderful that he had lived so long' marvelled Barker.

He was buried the following Sunday after divine service. The coffin was borne by six soldiers and the pall bearers were Dr Davis, Mr Owen, Mr Hickey, and Captain Barker. The rough-sawn box was draped with black silk, and Radford's military hat and sword were laid on top. Dr Wilson was the chief mourner, followed by Radford's servant, Donohoe*, who had been denied the right to bear the coffin, despite being 'much attached to his master'. Dr Wilson wrote that Radford was buried with full 'military honours, and with great respect; every man, woman and child in the settlement attending, as he was much beloved' (Wilson, 1835).

Despite the death of his friend, Wilson settled into life at the fort and related the story of the final months of the settlement in his book†. He was a well-respected Naval gentleman, and, by 1836,

---

*   Of Donohoe, little is known after this. He was returned to New South Wales and granted a Ticket of Leave in June 1830 and was freed a month later. He then probably lived in Sydney until his death, in June 1838, at the age of 35. He is buried at the 'Seven Mile Hollow Stockade' (Street, 2012).

†   By the time Raffles Bay was abandoned on 31 August, Wilson had lived at the fort for two months. He then travelled with Barker to the new Swan River colony in Western Australia, and became an explorer of the King George Sound area (Albany), naming Mount Barker after his friend. He returned to England but continued his travelling life. In total he made nine journeys to Australia, and was the first to introduce, among other things, European honey bees to Tasmania. He was granted 5000 acres of land in a district of New South Wales, which was named after him: Braidwood. He bought 4000 more acres and became a successful pastoralist for several years, until the 1840s drought led him to bankruptcy. He

a member of the Royal Geographical Society. A full review of his book was presented in the February 1836 edition of *The Monthly Review*, and the author, Ralph Griffiths, wrote in awe of the success of the shipwrecked survivors of the *Governor Ready* and delighted at Wilson's evaluation of the 'savages'. Wilson considered most of the Europeans who came into contact with Aborigines along the coast of New Holland were 'lawless vagabonds, whose treatment of the aborigines is unjust and cruel in the extreme' and people therefore needed to discount their evaluations and recommendations. Griffiths was pleased that at last, empathetic Europeans, like Wilson and Captain Barker, were arriving in Australia to deal with Aboriginal people with humanity and consideration (Griffiths, February 1836).

Wilson was a man of his times, however humanitarian, and would order the required number of lashes for convict miscreants when necessary. In the appendices of his book, he gives advice to other doctors about how to manage Crown Prisoners. His 'chief maxim' was:

> ... *never to permit the slightest slang expression to be used, nor flash songs to be sung, nor swearing; while indecent language is punished with unrelenting severity ... (Wilson, 1835).*

Wilson's prisoners were to remain miserable. He would not permit 'dancing, wrestling, or, indeed, any amusement to take place among' them, although he rarely ordered his prisoners to be flogged. He didn't have to, he said, because of the 'decorum, cleanliness, and quietness' he insisted upon. His alternative punishments included long lectures *without* the right of reply, parading the deck for four or eight hours with 'his bed tied to his back' and standing on deck, staring aft, 'without permission to speak, or be spoken to'. There was one exception in his use of corporal punishment, however, which might please modern comedians and radio show hosts:

---

died in 1843 and is buried on a hill overlooking the town that now stands on the western end of his lands and bears his name.

... There is, however, a class of prisoners, that, unless narrowly looked after, frequently occasion a great deal of disturbance. I allude to attorneys' clerks, of which class of the community I have, in all my voyages, had a considerable number. The few instances in which I have been compelled to inflict corporal punishment, have been on these gentry, to whom I show no mercy, if detected in fomenting disturbances; and I have invariably found, that flogging a lawyer has a wonderful effect in preserving order among other prisoners ... (Wilson, 1835).

Chapter 6
The final month

In May and June 1829, unknown to the people in Fort Wellington, a famous little cutter, named *HMS Mermaid,* was already heading back north from Sydney with new orders for the settlement. They were to abandon the fort.

Influential men had read the sour reports of the early commandants, and the tyranny of distance and the slow speed of news did the rest. George Windsor Earl, who was a leading proponent of the next attempt at settlement in the north a decade later, blamed Captain Stirling, the founder of the fort, for being distracted by other pursuits (Earl, 1846). Since leaving Raffles Bay, Stirling had become the commandant of the new settlement of Swan River, in Western Australia. Earl wrote that Stirling's report on the Swan River was so favourable he convinced the government to:

> ... *colonise the country in its neighbourhood; and as it was supposed that a commercial enterprise with the Indian Islands could be carried on as advantageously from the Swan River as from Raffles Bay, an establishment at the latter place was of course deemed to be no longer necessary* ... *(Earl, 1846)*

Anyway, the little northern settlements were not without controversy in Sydney either, as editorials in *Australian* showed:

> ... *Orders have arrived from England for the immediate abandonment of Port Raffles. Thus, another of our sweet, nice, wise, profitable, gingerbread, out of the way playthings, is to go to pot, after the many thousand pounds spent upon it, the many hands, and the productive labor of which it has helped to impoverish New*

South Wales. Long ago did we shew the absurdity, the futility, the injurious tendency of these new settlements. Still the rage went on. Something must be done with Port Wellington and Port Raffles and Western Port, and King George's Sound—they afforded nice sugar plums for Commandants and Engineers, and Superintendents. There was a 'great cry', but 'very, little wool'. So, one is abandoned, and another abandoned, and still some are hanging on. This judicious order of the Ministers, which tallies so exactly with all we have affirmed and all we have urged, is to snap short the frail thread of Port Raffles ... (Australian, *12 May 1829).*

And three days later:

... The Government schooner Mermaid is to proceed immediately with necessaries and orders, but no more mechanics, to Port Raffles, in order to prepare our gingerbread plaything there for abandonment. The Mermaid, we hear, after calling at Port Raffles, and another of our important possessions in the same quarter, styled Port Essington, is meant to proceed across the Gulf of Carpentaria, and calling at Swan Port to leave provisions subsequently at another of our nice, snug, profitable, good for nothing, mock establishments, King George's Sound, making the passage back to Port Jackson round Van Diemen's Land, or through Bass' Straits, and thus performing a circumnavigation of New Holland ... (Australian, *15 May 1829).*

The *Mermaid** knew these waters well. She had first been to the northern coasts with Phillip Parker King during his surveys of 1818 and 1820. King had named the islands and landmarks he discovered after notable Englishmen of the day. Raffles Bay was named after Sir Stamford Raffles on 16th of April 1820, the year after he founded Singapore. King was in Raffles Bay long enough to paint the *Mermaid* lying peacefully in its waters, and *Mermaid Shoals*, north of Apsley Strait in the Tiwi Islands, carries the ship's name to this day.

The *Mermaid* was back in May 1826, bringing buffaloes from Timor to Fort Dundas, under Captain Samual John Dowsett. She

---

* 'The *Mermaid* was with the *Lady Nelson* and the *Prince Regent*, when Captain Allman established Port Macquarie in April 1821. She was then used for further exploration work, taking John Oxley up the Queensland coast where they discovered and charted the Brisbane River, Moreton Bay, and Stradbroke Island and identified a suitable site for a new convict settlement there.

Figure 13: *Mermaid* at Endeavour River (FL1032663 SLNSW).

arrived the day after the *Isabella*, with Major Campbell and members of the 57th Regiment of Foot aboard, to take over from the 3rd Regiment. *HMS Mermaid* was to be the replacement for the *Lady Nelson*, which was taken by pirates in the islands to the north of Australia. The *Mermaid* undertook several supply runs to Timor, bringing more buffaloes, cattle, pigs, grains and other stores to the settlement and, on the establishment of Fort Wellington, she transferred men and equipment from Melville Island to Raffles Bay. She was then relieved by the *Mary Elizabeth* and returned sick and injured men to Sydney:

> ... *The Colonial Government Schooner* Mermaid, *which arrived from the Northward yesterday, brings most disastrous accounts of hardships in various ways, and mortality, suffered at the settlements of Melville Island and Port Essington. Among the deaths at Melville Island, is included that of Dr. Wood, staff surgeon. There is not now any medical man on either of the two settlements; that duty is performed by a Lieutenant in the army. She brings to Sydney a great number of persons in a sickly state, from Melville Island, and Raffles Bay. Reports that all hands at the latter place are in a shocking condition with the scurvy, &c ... (Australian, 22 Feb 1828).*

In May 1829, it was the *Mermaid*, then under Captain Samuel Nolbrow, that was chosen to return to Raffles Bay to carry Governor Darling's new orders for the settlement. These were instructions for the abandonment of Fort Wellington and the transfer of men, stock and equipment to the Swan River colony in Western Australia.

But in June, whilst the *Mermaid* sailed north through the reefs of Queensland, John Radford was still shopping in Timor. With Nolbrow possibly drunk at the wheel and choosing, against orders, a reckless inner route through the Torres Strait reefs, she struck the coral near the Frankland Islands, and went down in a matter of minutes (SBS, 2019). After a stellar 13-year career, the gallant little ship had run out of luck, and she was ignominiously abandoned to the reef. Nolbrow and his crew endured 11 days in small boats before they were picked up by *HMS Admiral Gifford*. A few days later they were transferred to a 335-ton brig named *HMS Swiftsure*, which was heading towards Raffles Bay. Nolbrow continued to guard the Governor's despatches desperately—he had saved nothing else, not even, to his humiliation, the ship's log. Then, on 4 July the *Swiftsure* was also wrecked on an unchartered reef off Cape Sidmouth in Queensland. Fortunately, the brig *Resource** was nearby. The crew of the *Swiftsure* and, what now must have been the very weary men of the *Mermaid*, were again rescued from small boats.

The *Resource* sailed through the rest of the reefs and reached Raffles Bay without further incident, and at last, Captain Nolbrow was

* There is some confusion as to the right name for this brig. Wilson called her Resource; *others say* Reserve *or* Resilience. *She was en route to the Isle of France from Sydney. The* Sydney Gazette, *on 26 November 1829, was even more confused and had little idea of the truth: their story had Captain Nolbrow wrecked in the* Mermaid, *the* Swiftsure, *the* Governor Ready, *the* Comet *and the* Jupiter, *all within about two weeks. Nolbrow, someone wrote, was 'singularly unfortunate, more so than we ever remember to have heard of in the instance of any surviving shipwrecked mariner.' (*Sydney Gazette, *26 Nov 1828, page 3). All these ships* were *wrecked in the Torres Strait that season, plus others, and even the* Resource *ran aground, although she got off without damage. Also, the* Governor Phillip *lost two anchors, and the* Thompson *lost her windlass (*Australian *25 Nov 1829 p3) (see Appendix 2).*

rowed ashore, clutching the Governor's despatches to his bosom. He was relieved to hand them over to the commandant of Fort Wellington, on 29 July 1829. Nolbrow later tried to salvage some of his reputation via a letter to the *Colonial Times* in Hobart, informing all of the 'perils of the sea' through a litany of ship disasters (see Appendix 5).

Captain Barker was shocked to get the order to abandon the settlement. In fact, he hesitated before obeying, because everything, at last, was going well. Darling and the government had made their decisions based on out-of-date information and Barker was sure that, if they knew the truth, the orders for abandonment would be countermanded. There were three reasons stated for the leaving the north: the 'unhealthiness of the climate'; the hostility of the natives; and the non-visitation of the Malays. All three were now overcome.

Captain Laws of the *Satellite*, and Dr Wilson had both been surprised and pleased with the health of the settlers. With better nutrition, starting when Sleeman was in command, the health of the men had improved, and it was clear that the climate was not a problem. At a time when visiting the contemporary settlements of Batavia (Jakarta) and Koepang (Kupang) meant a high chance of dying from one of the fevers or other maladies that plagued them, the small communities on the north coast of New Holland had the potential to prove ideal environments for health.

And, by 1829, the natives were no longer hostile. Captain Barker's perseverance in his attempts to learn as much as he could about the traditional owners of the land he was occupying had paid huge dividends: the Iwaidja were now welcoming. Dr Wilson concluded that:

> ... the hostility of the natives was caused or ... aggravated by the conduct of the settlers; and that as soon as conciliatory measures were adopted, their hostility ceased ... (Wilson, 1835).

Wellington and his clan may have been sorry to see the British go. They were more than a source of iron nails and other resources;

the tiny settlement was also novel and entertaining, and Barker and Wilson were friends. The irony of this, after such a dismal start in inter-race relations, is patent, but the same thing happened two decades later as the Port Essington settlement of Victoria was abandoned. Then, women wailed and cut themselves with stones in grief and, as Don Christopherson, a modern historian from the Muran Clan of Western Arnhem Land, said: 'there are some amazing stories of Aboriginal people and the British treating each other with respect... If people are going to stand on the beach and cry for you, and have sorrow in their hearts, they must have had a good relationship' (Moodie, 2019).

Lastly, the Malays were now visiting Raffles Bay in considerable numbers, and more were planning to come, aware that there was now protection from coastal peoples. When Barker and Wilson were in Koepang after leaving Raffles Bay, they heard from the captain of the *Mercus* that there were groups of Chinese people in Java, preparing to emigrate to Fort Wellington, and that they 'had anticipated great advantages from commercial intercourse' there.

Barker's hesitation after reading the orders was brief. He was, after all, a soldier. He ordered all building work to be stopped, as he was required to, and quickly wrote to the Dutch Governors in Java and Macassar, asking them to pass on the news that there was no longer any British in northern Australia. It would have been unfortunate for trepang fishermen to invest in trade goods they could no longer trade, or for immigrants to arrive at an abandoned settlement.

> *... I have the honor to acquaint you that this Settlement is about to be abandoned, instructions to that effect having been received from the Secretary of State. It being, I conceive, of importance that the Macassar fishermen and traders should be aware of our removal ... (Barker, 12 August 1829).*

The day before the orders had arrived, three other ships had dropped anchor in Raffles Bay. The *Amity*, under Lieutenant Owen, the frigate *HMS Satellite*, under Captain Laws, which had visited

Figure 14: Mr Weston's sketch of the Iwaidja dancing. Dr Wilson is on the left, and Dr Davis claps time, on the right. The pea-shooter sized didgeridoo the seated man is playing is too small to make low sounds, but a skilled player could play a lively rhythm using it (Source: Wilson, 1834).

the settlement in 1828, and the *Reliance* under Captain Hays. On board the *Reliance* with Captain Hays and his wife, were Lieutenant Weston, an officer if the East India Company, and Major Cuppage, who were en route to Singapore. Suddenly, Barker was surrounded by his social equals and, unsurprisingly, a party was planned. *HMS Satellite* had just returned from the South Pacific, and the crew had collected an array of Taheitan [sic] clothing, feathered hats, drums, clubs, carvings, shells, and other things that were 'curiosities' to Barker, and a high time was had examining them all.

On 3 August, Barker recorded that he dined with Captain Laws and his officers, and Mr Weston and Mr Gray with 'much satisfaction'. Dr Wilson was there too, of course, and he was reunited with several old ship mates, which recalled for him 'the days of *Auld Lang Syne*'.

The next day the visitors were again in the camp, and so too were Wellington and 22 other Aborigines. Dr Wilson was enthralled, as usual, and this can be seen in the sketch Mr Weston drew of Wilson and Dr Davis amid a crowd of dancing Iwaidja. Wilson has his arms around the shoulders of two men, and Davis claps along to the rhythm of a small didgeridoo*. Wilson published the sketch in his 1834 book, describing it as 'a very spirited and correct sketch of this singular performance.' Davis hadn't improved on his rhythm attempts of the previous January, because:

> ... although he might keep time correctly enough for a civilised ball-room, yet he fell short in that necessary part, at least to a savage ear; so they, in very polite terms, requested that he not fatigue himself, but stand and look at them ... (Wilson, 1835).

The loss of the *Mermaid* was a serious blow to Barker's ability to transport stock, stores and people to the new colonies on the Swan River and at King George's Sound. Fortunately, however, a brig named *Thompson* was in the bay. She was a private ship, under a 35-year-old master, Captain John Hobbs. Commander Laws of the *Satellite* suggested that Barker charter the *Thompson* for transport, and within days he and Barker had drawn up a 'Charter Party' with Hobbs, for a lease of '£400 & £45 for dunnage† if not taken to Swan River'. In the event that another government ship arrived and could be used for transport, the Charter Party would be cancelled, and Hobbs paid just £45, or, as it was stated in the legal English necessary:

> ... PROVIDED ALSO and it is hereby agreed between the said parties that, in case the said Vessel shall not be required to proceed on the aforesaid voyage the said Commander J. M. Laws and Captain Barker, on behalf of His Majesty, His Heirs and Successors, do agree to pay for the detention of the said vessel until the sixteenth inst. inclusive The sum of Forty five pounds by Navy Bills in the Customary manner and then and in that ease the aforesaid covenant to pay Four Hundred pounds shall be void and of no effect ... (Barker, 7 August 1829).

When the order came to abandon the settlement, there was much to organise in a very short time. The Iwaidja were among

---

* D'Urville described such an instrument at Victoria Settlement in 1840: 'Young M. Bremer ... taking a long flute of the natives, pierced with a hole into which they blow with the nose, he undertook to perform...' (d'Urville, 1839).

† 'Dunnage' is loose wood or matting used to hold cargo in position in a ship's hold.

Barker's first thoughts and he made it clear to the men how they would be leaving the settlement:

... Gave orders to 57th, the Mili[tary] and Crown Prisns to destroy nothing of either buildings or fences & to leave everything that I do not consider worth taking for materials, just as it stands. ...

Despite his workload, Barker felt it important to take a final opportunity to learn more about the Iwaidja, by visiting and exploring Croker Island. He borrowed the yawl from the *Satellite*, a better boat than the settlement ever owned, and sailed into Bowen Strait with Captain Laws, Dr Wilson, Dr Davis and Mr Cleary for an overnight journey. The boat dropped them on Croker Island, then sailed south for a later rendezvous, whilst the men crossed a vast treeless plain on foot. They named it *Laws' Plain*, took samples of soil and noted freshwater sources. They met several Iwaidja, who were 'quite children', who walked with them. Re-joining the boat, they sailed further south and then met Mago and Wadyere, and others, in canoes and re-landed to spend the evening with them around the fire, singing and dancing until after 10 p.m., when they left to sleep on board the boat.

The next day they took soundings and mapped Bowen Strait, before returning to Raffles Bay, and the *Satellite* departed for India the next morning. On board were the marines left by *HMS Success* two years before. Their tour of duty was up, and they were at last heading home (Wilson, 1835).

For the Crown Prisoners, abandoning the fort meant the likelihood of being returned to hard labour, or worse situations, in the southern part of Australia, where escape was impossible. The *Amity* and chartered transport ship, *Thompson*, were to take all the Crown Prisoners left in Raffles Bay to King George's Sound, on 23 August 1829. The islands only a few days to the north offered opportunity, and four men had already made their escape to them after stealing a boat.

The temptation of escape was high for men who felt they had nothing to lose, and this included Matthew Carr and Robert Craggs. The idea went around that anyone left behind by the *Thompson,* on 23 August, would be able to live freely at the fort until they could work out how to escape—possibly by getting a lift on a Macassan prau at the end of the trepang season, or as Mr Hickey, the storekeeper suggested, by 'taking' the *Governor Phillip** which was yet to arrive. The blacksmith, James Smith, had been excluded from a conversation at Henry Langton's house, but he overheard it, and was willing to tell Barker that Carr and Craggs had discussed stealing a boat and escaping with several others: Kelly, Potts, Richards, Sellers and William Philips (Street, 2012). They were all then arrested and held on the *Thompson,* under guard, until departure time. Corporal Clay overheard them talking about their plan one evening in the *Thompson's* bow: Craggs was disappointed that they would now no longer be in a position to steal the whale boat and 'must give it all up'. Ironically, this may have saved their lives, as most lived for many years afterwards.

Henry Langton was one of those most interested in this type of talk. He was a ship's clerk who had been sent down, for life, for forgery in 1817. A tall blonde 19-year-old youth, he was well educated and intelligent, and must have cursed his luck when transported to Sydney in the *Shipley*. He arrived with 124 other prisoners on 24 April 1817 and served his punishment in a variety of roles and places, including as a constable, and a clerk, in both Windsor and Newcastle. It's hard to see that his work was particularly onerous, but by the mid-1820s, Langton was getting in trouble for being a 'runaway from Government employment' and being out after hours (Street, 2012). When he volunteered for Raffles Bay, his skills as a clerk ensured his recruitment. By then, he was a 30-year-old experienced

---

* This was always unlikely but, to be sure, Barker intended to float warning letters in different parts of the bay so she would not be taken by surprise. In the end, the *Governor Phillip* arrived two days later without incident (Journal 18 August 1829).

lag, and he became the Overseer and Clerk for Fort Wellington and a trusted worker, particularly by Barker, whose journal mentions him regularly. He kept the accounts and the meteorological returns, and as first overseer, was in charge of all the prisoners. When the orders came telling Barker to abandon the fort, and take the settlers and equipment to the new settlement in King George's Sound, Langton's position and status were threatened.

The *Governor Phillip,* under Captain Drysdale, was expected any day. It would take many days to load everything on board the ships, and each day's work had to start early. On 24 August, the *Thompson's* boats were beached in preparation for loading at 4 a.m., and Barker expected to hear the convicts beginning. It remained quiet:

> … *On going down to enquire the reason, the Overseer was not to be found. Set Adams, the second Overseer to superintend the loading. It was soon ascertained that Langton had gone off into the bush in the night, and that Mr Hickey's servant, Fellows, was also gone and had taken his gun. It seemed to be imagined that they had an intention of living in the woods till the Malays arrived and then going with them. The Overseer has left us at a very awkward time, but we must put our shoulders to the wheel … (Barker, Journal 1829).*

Langton and Fellows gave it their best shot, but after a few days they gave themselves up—just before the *Governor Phillip* departed the bay for good.

> … *Langton and Fellows gave themselves up this morning … He {Fellows} had suffered much and could hardly stand. Langton also much fagged. Sent them to the cells … (Barker, Journal 1829).*

Langton was to rue the day further, even after his term at King George's Sound was over. In Hyde Park Barracks, in November 1830, he asked to be paid the balance of a small salary due to him as First Overseer and Clerk at Fort Wellington, but found the government had a long memory. His salary was forfeited, he was told, as soon as he had absconded (Street, 2012).

Thomas Fellows didn't do much better, but he may have learned more about surviving in the bush. He later absconded from King

Figure 15: A 1975 replica of the *Amity* on display in King George's Sound, now Albany, W.A. (SLWA 133698PD).

George's Sound and, this time, lasted seven months before giving himself up. In and out of trouble, it wasn't until 1849, 20 years later, that Fellows finally managed to earn a conditional pardon.

In the last few days before departure, the temptation to seek freedom by hiding in the bush and waiting for the Macassans to come remained, and other long-term Crown Prisoners also gave it a go:

> ... *four others also absconded on the 17th and 18th. I could not have prevented it without taking measures that would have too much harassed my men. It is not easy to state positively what were their views ... (Barker, 22 August 1829).*

The four included Belgian sailor, Joseph van Hammett and John Tobin, who absconded the night after Langton, and Zacharia Trueman and Michael Dwyer, a couple of nights later. Dwyer survived

118

on cockles for three days, whilst waiting to be joined by Trueman 'on the flat', before hunger drove him back to the fort. John Tobin lasted three days as well, and returned, without van Hammett, 'in a miserable state', but in time to be transferred to King George's Sound. Tobin was either 'simple or a very cunning fellow, but I believe the former & has been worked on by others' wrote Barker*.

Of what became of Trueman and van Hammett, nothing is known. They were never seen again.

One instruction which gave Barker pain was to leave the little Iwaidja girl, Reveral, behind. Reveral now only spoke English and would barely interact with the Iwaidja, when they visited. Plus, she showed such a clear preference to stay with the Littles, that Barker disobeyed the order and let her accompany them to King George's Sound, stating:

> ... since I received your communication of the 27th June, I
> have been unable to comply with its 2nd Paragraph, but I feel
> convinced that his Excellency will approve of my not doing so and
> of my allowing the native girl to leave the settlement ...

Barker claimed that Reveral's family wanted her to leave with the British:

> ... She has the greatest abhorrence of being left, and the natives
> so far from wishing it, have asked me to take her, and seemed
> much pleased when I consented, evidently from a feeling that she
> would be well taken care of and much better off than with them.
> They kissed and seemed to take leave of her this morning before
> she went on board. They express much sorrow at our going ...
> (Barker, Journal 1829).

On Saturday, 22 August 1829, when Reveral was boarding the *Thompson* on the day before departure, her countrymen 'shook hands with her very affectionately, and appeared much pleased with, though somewhat envious of, her good fortune'.

---

* Tobin had been shipped to New Holland on the *Mangles* with Dr Wilson in charge as the surgeon. Wilson was therefore able to vouch for him as 'simple'. Tobin was Welsh and, on the voyage out, could 'not speak one word of English' (Wilson, 1835).

... She left the land of her fathers, not only without regret, but with much satisfaction, seemingly delighted to be out of the reach of her sable kindred, towards whom she invariably evinced great shyness, and even antipathy ... (Wilson, 1835).

Wellington asked to go on board the *Thompson* the next day to see the girl but was 'diverted from his purpose' and none of the Iwaidja ever saw her again. She was last recorded as arriving in Sydney in 1830, and what happened to her after that is unknown, although, as historian Barbara James suggests, Reveral probably accompanied William Little and his wife, and young George, when the 39th Regiment sailed for Madras, in 1832, thereby passing 'out of the annals of Australian history' (James, 1989). Hopefully, she was not one of the 11 children of the Regiment to die of cholera during the Madras posting.

On 24 August, the *Amity* and the *Thompson* finally set sail and departed Raffles Bay, heading around the coast to King George's Sound. On board were most of the men, the stock and stores, and the little girl, Reveral.

These days, the good folk of Albany, in Western Australia, so reveer the contribution made by the *Amity*, that the town boasts a replica of her in dry-dock.

Barker remained with Dr Wilson, Serjeant Drew, several Crown Prisoners (including Dwyer, who had given up his attempt to escape), and the remaining soldiers of the 39th, and several days were spent cutting hay for the last remaining animals who would travel with them on the *Governor Phillip*. They also pulled down the officers' cottage, the cells, and the blacksmith's forge, and loaded the building materials on board.

Barker loaded his own baggage on 26 August, and then took Mago, and several others, into the gardens and:

... pointed out which plants & fruits were eatable. One of the bananas was ripening & I gave them some which they appeared very fond of ...

He also 'turned loose: 1 cock, 2 hens, 5 chickens', but they probably didn't survive long. Other animals left behind certainly did:

already the buffaloes and pigs, cats and rats they had brought were spreading out across the Top End unchecked.

Barker left the settlement to his Iwaidja friends and declared:

... We leave this place on a perfectly friendly footing with the natives ...

The last of the British boarded the ship on 28 August, although they didn't depart until the next morning, after Barker returned to the beach, took his usual morning bathe, and arranged the nailing of the 'old colours to the Flagstaff at the Fort' as a final act. Captain Drysdale was given his sailing orders and when, at last, the *Governor Phillip* was under way, the fort was 'abandoned to Wellington'.

They left behind four of the garrison in lonely graves: the convict William Leak; Dr Wood; Mr Radford; and an unnamed infant. They weren't the only people buried during the two years of settlement*. Two crewmen of the *Amity* lay beside them in the cemetery. William Collins and William Erasmus died from fever contracted in Koepang on 2 and 3 July 1829 (Wilson, 1835).

There were others who were not counted among the 'official' losses of the settlement because their fates were unknown: Private John Cook, who disappeared after a mental breakdown, and later, Zacharia Trueman and Joseph van Hammett who fled into the bush, were never seen again, and they ended their lives who knows where. Several Macassans died near the settlement too: Barker noted that a Malay from the *Pattie Djawaija* was 'buried in the sand near Bathing Point without any ceremony' on 8 May. Also, the data he collected from the 1053 Malay crew from the 30 praus that arrived during the 1829 trepang season, shows there were 40 deaths among them (Mulvaney & Green, 1992).

Remarkably, the Iwaidja suffered little during Barker's time as commandant. Hartwig compared him to other settlement leaders:

... Probably the most telling illustration of the importance of Barker and his approach to inter-racial relations was that, under

---

* Thirty-three men and women had been buried in the Top End soil outside Fort Dundas, so in terms of lives, Fort Wellington had been far less expensive.

his administration at Raffles Bay and later at Albany in Western Australia, no Aboriginal deaths, or even injuries, resulted from aggression by his troops or the convicts in his care. How different this statistic is when compared to the many violent conflicts reported in the literature occurring in other regions of the new colonies from the arrival of the First Fleet in 1788 ... (Hartwig, 2007).

One of Dr Wilson's last acts was to install a gravestone, which had been sent from Sydney via the *Satellite*, on Dr Cornelius Wood's grave.

Two years later, the Secretary for War and Colonies, Viscount Goderich, announced that the government had saved £761 annually by closing Fort Dundas and Fort Wellington, 'exclusive of the expense of maintaining communications between those settlements and Sydney' (Graham, 1967).

Barker travelled to the Swan River and King George's Sound on the *Governor Phillip*, calling in at Koepang, both to settle accounts and revictual for the coming voyage. They were there a little longer than planned, because:

... We lost two days at Koepang from the Ship's crew being much out of order and continually drunk when sent on shore ... (Barker, 23 October 1829).

In King George's Sound, he took over from Lieutenant Sleeman and worked hard to develop the community, despite the desire of the new Governor of the Swan River colony, James Stirling, for Western Australia to remain a 'free colony', without convict labour*. When, on 7 March 1831, King George's Sound was declared to be a part of the Swan River colony, the military and their convict charges once again had to abandon their settlement and return to New South Wales. Barker had been successful in his cross-cultural relationships with the Aborigines of both Raffles Bay and King George's Sound,

---

* In 1838 John Lort Stokes enjoyed the irony of approaching Fremantle and the Swan River colony in the *Beagle*: the most conspicuous building was a gaol that was 'rather a singular Pharos for a settlement in Australia which boasts its uncontaminated state' (Hordern, 1989).

and Governor Darling recognised his exceptional qualities. Darling thought Barker would achieve great things in the new colony of New Zealand, as he was 'eminently' qualified to 'conciliate and manage the Natives, while likely to restore mutual racial confidence' (Mulvaney, 1993).

Unfortunately, Barker never made it to New Zealand, and history took a different route. No doubt looking forward to his promotion, he boarded the *Isabella*, and headed towards Sydney with orders to explore the mouth of the River Murray on the way. There, he lost his life …

Lieutenant-Colonel White, of the 39th Regiment, tells the story of what happened:

> … *They eventually reached the hillock where three years earlier Sturt had pitched his tent. They moved on until they found the channel by which the Murray reached the sea. This channel appeared to be about a quarter of a mile wide. Barker was determined to swim this channel: his companions were much against this decision, as they could not swim. But Barker was very keen to make observations of this territory where no white man had ever set foot before. He set out alone with his compass strapped to his head. His party saw him land and ascend a small hillock, from which he waved his last farewell, as from that moment he disappeared completely.*
>
> *A sharp cry was vaguely heard by one of his party. The survivors passed an anxious night but were able to do nothing.*
>
> *Years later an old black woman gave some details of Barker's murder. His compass caused the natives some consternation, but if only he had gone to meet them in his nakedness, instead of turning back, they would not have treated him as hostile. They assailed him with spears, and at the water's edge, this old crone said, he turned to face his adversaries, and received a spear in his chest, which killed him instantly.*
>
> *A memorial was erected in 1903 by the residents of Mount Barker … (White, 1955).*

Why Barker was killed is a matter of conjecture. Throughout the 1830s, a number of sealers based themselves at a camp on Kangaroo

Figure 16: Collet Barker's memorial tablet at St. James' Church Sydney (SLSA PRG 280143220).

Island. They were lawless and violent men, not adverse to killing Aborigines or stealing Aboriginal women. A lone white man found in the sand dunes may have offered an opportunity for revenge the Aborigines couldn't miss. Or, as Captain Sturt suggested, the 'natives who perpetrated the deed, were influenced by no other motive than curiosity to see if they had power to kill a white man'. This is possible, though not probably. Sturt's description of the killing is also conjecture, as there were no witnesses, other than the killers:

> ... Captain Barker tried to soothe them, but finding that they were determined to attack him, he made for the water, from which he could not have been very distant. One of the blacks immediately threw his spear and struck him in the hip. This did not, however, stop him. He got among the breakers, when he received the second spear in his shoulder. On this, turning round he received a third spear full in the breast; with such deadly precision do these savages cast their weapons. It would appear that the third spear was already on its flight, when Captain Barker turned, and it is to be hoped, that it was at once mortal. He fell on his back in the water. The natives then rushed in, and dragging him out by the legs, seized their spears, and inflicted innumerable wounds upon his body; after which, they threw it in the deep water, and the sea tide carried it away ... (Sturt, 1835).

Vale Captain Collet Barker, 1784–1831.

Chapter 7
And now?

Fort Wellington was abandoned nearly 200 years ago, and people have visited the site only rarely since then. There is no record of how many, of course, but the Iwaidja continued to live in the region, Macassan trepangers continued to visit the coast, pearlers and fishermen harvested the bay, and yachties and other wayfarers anonymously passed through. Few had any reason other than a passing interest to go to the site, although the Iwaidja probably 'mined' metal and glass from the site for many years, reworking pieces of each into useful implements, or tools, like they did after the closure of Victoria Settlement in 1849 (Allen, 1973).

Luckily, some of the travellers published articles or journals of their exploits, and there were a few nineteenth century buffalo hunters who left signs of temporary occupation. I was keen to visit the site myself and record my own observations, but as there is no road access through the modern Garig Gunak Barlu National Park, the only choice is by sea. For a while I thought I could get there relatively easily, relying on friends with boats, but unfortunately, a coronavirus disrupted the world at just the wrong time and, rightly, travel through Aboriginal lands anywhere was no longer possible. My visit would have to wait, and my experience would remain second-hand through the records which have been left by visitors to the site.

When Victoria Settlement was established in Port Essington in 1838, Lieutenant P.B. Stewart of the *Britomart*, in his 'decked-boat', was sent to report on Fort Wellington's condition. After ten years of cycles of the tropical climate, the ravages of termites and bushfires, his report was not encouraging.

Then, about the same time, the first visitor from foreign lands to come was the remarkable traveller, Captain Jules Sébastien César Dumont d'Urville, leading a French scientific expedition. Captain d'Urville was the same man who had preceded Stirling in his exploration of the Swan River in 1827. His 1839 expedition, consisting of two ships, the *Astrolabe* and the *Zélée*, spent eight days in Raffles Bay, in April. The French scientists set up an observatory on a small island the Englishmen had called Second Island, but naturally, they were curious about the settlement and went to find it, although 'from the anchorage, nothing indicated where this settlement might have been':

> *… every side of the shore presented a uniform appearance … I set off … in the whaler to explore the bay and look for the site of the English settlement. We had only gone southeast … about a mile and a half when we saw a section of wall still outstanding …*
> *We came ashore without seeing any trace of a landing stage, but the sea was so flat that the boats would come up to shore with no danger, under enormous trees which leant an air of coolness to the beach and which contrasted to the general appearance of the land. We then made out a space clear of timber and completely covered by long grass. This must have been the position of the fort, but there were no other remains of it, except that we saw a very thick wall in ruins, which I suppose was a powder magazine.*
> *We also saw the remains of an old forge and a well of brackish water. As for the gardens which, according to their accounts, the English had left, we looked in vain for traces of them, but all had vanished. Without doubt the natives had made frequent visits to this place after the departure of the British and they had materially hastened the destruction of what remained. Several graves that were protected against the attacks of the natives by a simple wooden fence had not been able to escape their investigations. The nails which had served to fasten the coffins had been the aim of the natives' greed and they had not been afraid to disturb the bodies to obtain these objects … (d'Urville, 1839).*

Barker no doubt would have been saddened to hear that the graves had been destroyed and disappointed that his carefully planted gardens and fruit trees hadn't even lasted a decade.

The French ships had been spotted by Macassan trepang fishermen on arrival. They immediately ran up their Dutch flags, continued into Port Essington, and reported their sightings to the officers in the British settlement of Victoria, established just six months earlier. Captain MacArthur immediately sent Lieutenant Stewart back to Raffles Bay, to see what the French were up to (Earl, 1846). Stewart found them busy taking mundane astrological measurements, collecting plant specimens, and filling their water tanks. There had been rumours, for decades, that the French were interested in the north coast of New Holland for themselves, but the lieutenant was convinced of d'Urville's scientific focus. Sir John Gordon Bremer invited d'Urville to dinner in the settlement, and d'Urville's journal gives us a valuable view of the new settlement through a visitor's eyes.

Several decades may have passed before more outsiders visited the Fort Wellington site. During the 1870s, a trio of buffalo hunters named Fred Dewar, Munro Leslie and Marshall, leased an expanse of land* between Raffles Bay and Mountnorris Bay (Bauer, 1964). They stayed only a season or two, but they easily harvested over a thousand buffalo hides in that time. They left behind 'permanent' structures, such as concrete water reservoirs and tanning cisterns, and there is a remnant fire hearth, of well-made bricks, still visible, that may have been in the kitchen of their homestead. All this confuses any modern research into the site, because the 1870's re-use, as Frederickson and de La Rue put it, 'introduces a complicating factor in identifying the date and purpose of several elements of the site's remaining physical fabric' (Frederickson & DeLaRue, 2013).

---

* A number of agricultural leases existed along this coast. For example, a man named Lewis leased land in Port Essington, for a cattle station, in the late 1870s. He was visited by Inspector Foelsche from the settlement at Port Darwin and photographs were taken.

The Historical Society of the Northern Territory (HSNT) made several expeditions to Fort Wellington, in an attempt to piece together the physical history of the site. The first expedition was in 1966, and its story was published in an entertaining little booklet, titled *Fort Wellington Raffles Bay* (HSNT, 1971). They found the remnants of walls and a couple of wells, one of which the ranger, Dave Lindner, climbed down to measure and take water samples, but they couldn't confirm the site of the fort:

> ... *The following days were spent in searching for further remains of the settlement, the stockade of the fort and the cemetery, with the gravestone of Dr. Cornelius Wood. We made an extensive but unsuccessful search for the gravestone. We failed to locate any remains of the stockade or fort. However, we are of the opinion that the fort and hexagonal stockade were situated on rising ground, slightly towards the east between the site of the remains of the buildings first discovered and the floor of the house on the promontory. It was in this site that we found a heap of bricks, which after having cleared away silt and leaves, we revealed a fireplace 62" X 4 3" made of two rows of bricks—two courses deep. From a corner of the fireplace a number of assorted nails were recovered in reasonably good condition. We believe that this could have been the fireplace attached to the Commandant's House within the stockade ... (HSNT, 1971).*

The Historical Society made a second expedition to the site, in 2009, to try and solve the 'enigma' of the fort's location (Reid, 2011). After several days of searching for artefacts, the members were satisfied that they had pinpointed it exactly: on the sand dunes below the promontory. Sitting around their camp fire, the expeditioners wondered at the wisdom of Stirling's thinking, 182 years earlier, when he chose the site. Lieutenant Sleeman had wondered the same thing in 1828, when he was designing a new fort to be built on the high ground, where Radford's cottage had been placed.

The shallow waters of the bay are easily accessible to boats, and they were used to farm cultured pearls before Cyclone Ingrid in 2005. Curious pearl farmers are likely to have explored the area. Also, wandering yachtsmen and souvenir hunters may have called in, unobserved, for decades. At Escape Cliffs, near the mouth of the Adelaide River, lie the remains of South Australia's first attempt at establishing Palmerston (1864–66). It is known that bottle collectors took everything valuable they could find from the site for decades, so it is likely some souvenir hunters also travelled to Fort Wellington to collect there (Pugh, 2018). Taking items from Raffles Bay has only been an offence since 2010, when it was finally listed on the Northern Territory Government's Heritage Register, because of its evident heritage value[*]:

> … *The Raffles Bay sites are of both national and Territory significance for a number of reasons. Established in 1827, Fort Wellington is one of the earliest settlements in Australia, and marks one of the earliest attempts to establish trade links with Asia. The experimental work conducted by the settlers in horticulture and agriculture make it one of the Territory's earliest agricultural sites.*
>
> *The Raffles Bay sites also have the archaeological potential to address issues relating to the antiquity of Macassan voyages to Australia, the distribution and characteristics of Macassan and non-Macassan trepanging sites, the nature of early European settlement in Australia and the nature of Aboriginal-Macassan contact and cultural exchange … (Gregory, 1996).*

Raffles Bay is still an isolated part of the Top End, made even more so by the closing of the vehicle tracks made by the Historical Society in previous years by the Garig Gunak Barlu National Park managers[†]. The park is managed through a partnership between the Parks and Wildlife Commission of the Northern Territory and the Traditional Owners of the land, through the Cobourg Peninsula Sanctuary and Marine Park Board.

Not much has changed in Raffles Bay over the last 200 years. It remains off sea lanes, few people ever visit, and its isolation makes

---

[*] Fort Dundas on Melville Island, the site of the first settlement north of Port Macquarie, is still not listed on the NT Government's Heritage Register.

[†] Note the term 'Garig'. This is a word that has been used to identify the dialect of the language spoken by the Iwaidja on the peninsula.

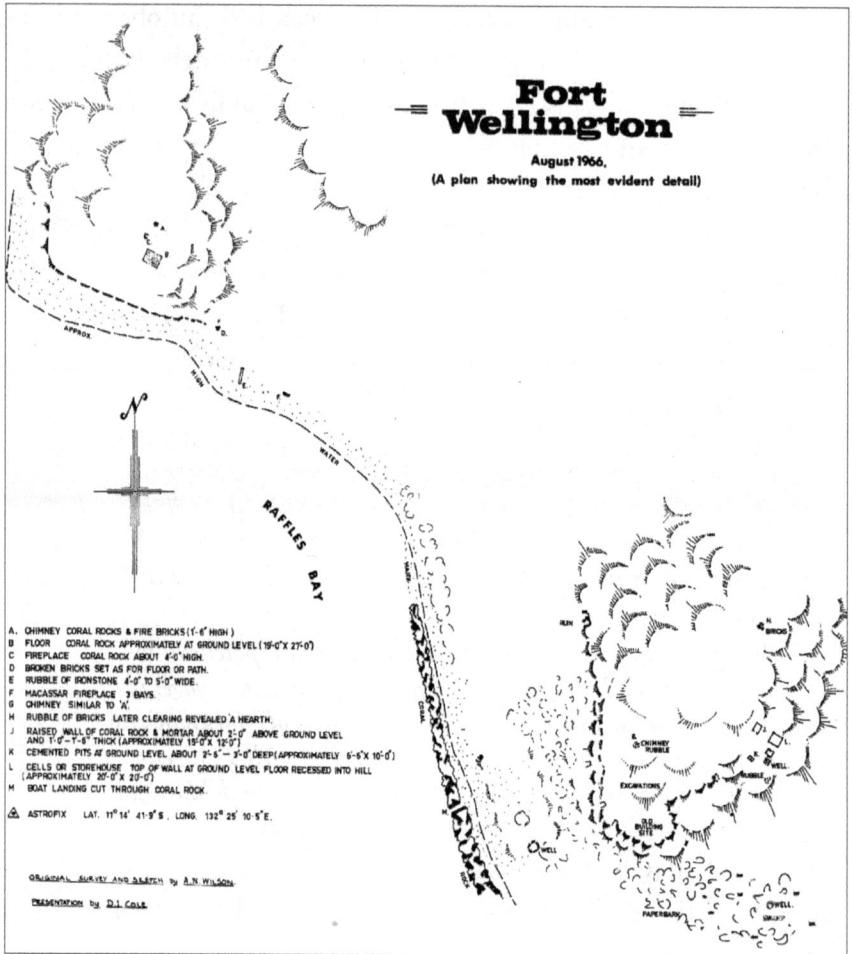

Map 3 Fort Wellington plan by A.N. Wilson, from 1966 (HSNT, 1971).

it unlikely that it will ever become a tourist attraction, despite its heritage listing.

An on-going mystery is the location of the cemetery. Dr Wilson installed a substantial carved gravestone on Dr Cornelius Wood's grave which has never been found. I suspect it has sunk into the sand after many dozens of tropical storms and lies there to this day just under the surface, waiting ...

Appendix 1
Lists of personnel

List of soldiers and marines who served at Fort Wellington

39th Regiment of Foot 1827–8

(Some soldiers were invalided out with scurvy during 1827–8)

Captain Henry Smyth
Lieutenant George Sleeman
Dr Cornelius Wood
Sergeant George Manyard
Sergeant Millwards and Mrs Millwards
Corporal John Hoop
Private George Knott (possibly corporal) and Mrs Knott
Lance-Corporal Daniel Turner
Private William Danks
Private Holland Stafford
Private Lewis
Private J Thomas

39th Regiment of Foot 1829	Captain Collet Barker
	Dr Robert Martin Davis (1798–1839)
	Lance-Sergeant Joseph Drew
	Lance-Sergeant John Shore
	Lance-Corporal Charles Clay
	Lance-Corporal William Parkes
	Lance-Corporal William McHugh
	Lance-Corporal James Shufflebottom
	Private John Asher
	Private William Carron
	Private William Collins
	Private William Connor
	Private John Cook and Mrs Cook
	Private Charles Duffield
	Private James Emms and Mrs Emms
	Private James Evans
	Private James Foley
	Private John Haigh
	Private William Harrison
	Private Richard Haslam and Mrs Haslam
	Mr E Hickey (storekeeper)
	Private John Higgins
	Private Phillip Lane
	Private Michael Leary
	Private William Little and Mrs Little
	Private Robert Meyers
	Private John Norton
	Private John Mills and Mrs Mills
	Private Michael Neale
	Private Michael Quinn
	Private Charles Shaves
	Private Joseph Sutton
	Private Richard Walsh
	Private Thomas Williams

Royal Marines, 1827–9	Sergeant Rob Webb, Corporal William Stagg Private Richard Medlicott Sergeant Thomas Harvey, Corporal Denham, Private Charles Bryant, Private Bullock Private Carson Private Hill Private Hodges Private Knott Private Denbow
57th Regiment (ex-Fort Dundas) 1829	Lance Corporal Henry Jesse Private John Dermott Private Edward Gollagher Private John Gleeson Private John Hoskins Private Thomas Sither Private Edward Sullivan

Table 2: Lists of Military at Fort Wellington (may be incomplete).
Sources: (Smyth, 1827 diary), (Wilson, 1835), (Mulvaney, 1993), (Barker, Journal 1829).

List of Crown Prisoners at Fort Wellington

Family[1] Name	Given Name	Age at court	Crime	Sentence	Occupation	Notes
Adams	Henry	23	Stealing lambs	life	Brick maker	Died 1857, aged 70, in Wee Waa.
Alexander	**William**	33	Homicide	14	Stone mason	Died 1857, aged 60, MacDonald River.
Auglin	**John**	23		7	Shoe maker	Aka Horace Quick/Quirk. Freed in 1831.
*Barry	John	40		7	Footman	Freed 1837.
Brady	Peter	19		7	Sawyer	Swan River and Port Arthur. Died 1870, aged 60, Dubbo.
Brennan	**Steven**	16	Stealing trousers	7	Stable boy	Freed 1834.
Brown	George	20	Breaking and entering, stealing	life	Ship and anchor smith	Aka Jerrit Healey. Probably died 1871, aged 63.
*Baldwin	Patrick	???				Freed 1827.
*Buckley	John					Returned to Sydney 21 Sept 1828 for health reasons.
Cahill	John	27	Murder	life	Cooper	Conditional pardon 1843. Died 1856, aged 55, Petersham.
Carr	Matthew	21	Fraud	life	Wheelwright	Died, 1832, aged 32, Norfolk Island.
*Carr	Thomas	28	Assault and theft	life	Sailor	Died 1837, aged 45, Sydney.
Clarke	Thomas	22	Burglary	7	Pit sawyer	Died 1856, aged 54, Camperdown.
Costello	Henry	19		7	Stockman	Died 1873, aged 68, Albury.

Family[1] Name	Given Name	Age at court	Crime	Sentence	Occupation	Notes
Craggs	Robert	20		life	Sawyer	Confined to ship *Thompson* with Sellers and Richards during preparations to abandon the fort in Aug 1827, as they were suspected of plotting to escape. Died 1852, aged 56, Parramatta.
*Cullen	Michael					Mentioned in letters by both Smyth and Barker.
Devine	Patrick	22	Sheep stealing	7	Miller and gardener	Freed 1831, married Ann Campbell 1834.
Donohoe	**Joseph**	20	Stealing lead	7	Servant	Died 1838, aged 35.
Doyle	**James**	16	Stealing handkerchiefs.	7	Cow boy	Freed 1832.
*Drumgold	Patrick			14	Gardener, nurseryman	Replaced Joseph Harrington who was returned to Sydney. Freed 1835. Died 1874, aged 83, Scone.
Dwyer	Michael		Burglary			Escaped on Aug 18, 1929 but returned the same evening. Also, for 4 days from King George's Sound in 1830, recaptured.
Fellowes	Thomas	22	Assault and theft	Life	Blacksmith	Pardoned 1849.
*Fitzgerald	John		Pickpocket	7	Servant	Servant to Lieut. Sleeman and transferred to King George's Sound with him.
Gibson	**James**	19	Stealing tobacco	7	baker	Freed 1830. Died 1874, aged 70, Liverpool.

135

Family[1] Name	Given Name	Age at court	Crime	Sentence	Occupation	Notes
*Godhead	Daniel	22	Burglary		Seaman / Sawyer	Returned to Sydney due to illness March 1828. Freed 1831.
*Harrington	Joseph	21	Stealing	7	Tailor	Worked as gardener. Returned to Sydney, sick, in early 1828.
Hassall	William Henry	44	?	Life	Seaman and navigator	Escaped by whaleboat on Oct 28, 1828, with Neal, Richardson and Wales. Never seen again but announced as died at sea.
Henrys	**William**	21	Burglary		Carpenter, tailor, pastry cook	Servant to Dr Gold until Gold's murder on Melville Island. Transferred to Ft Wellington. Died 1838, aged 34, Maitland.
Holt	**Charles**	20	Stealing 10 shawls	14	Painter and glazier	Servant to Major Ovens at Melville Island. Transferred to FW in 1829. Freed 1831.
Hoolahan	**William**	34	Stealing 4 bed sheets	7	Shoemaker	Transferred from Melville Island in 1829. Freed 1833.
Johnson	Andrew					No information, mentioned by Barker.
***Johnson**	**Robert**	22	Horse stealing	Life	Baker	Died 1856, age 49, Camperdown.
Kelly	**James**	33	Burglary	Life	Sailor	Pardoned 1848. Died 1853, aged 57 (?) Sydney.
*Landers	James		Burglary	Life	Shoemaker	

Family[1] Name	Given Name	Age at court	Crime	Sentence	Occupation	Notes
Langton	Henry	19	Forgery	Life	Clerk	Overseer of Convicts and Clerk of the Settlement at FW. Absconded for 3 days just before abandonment.
*Locke / Lack /Leek	William		Stealing lead	7		Sent as a free man and became second overseer. Died 23 April 1828 and mentioned by Sleeman as William 'Lack'.
Lockwood	William	28	Embezzlement	14	Clerk	
Maas	John Herman				Interpreter, copy clerk.	
Martin	Thomas			7	Blacksmith	Freed June 1830. Married Ann Smith.
McCarthy	**Michael**	14	Larceny		Plasterer's boy / gardener	Sent from Melville Island to be a gardener for Fort Wellington, awarded with Ticket of Leave. Died 1865, aged 59, Liverpool.
*McLellan	Joseph				Groom	Returned from FW sick in Feb 1828.
Mills	Joseph	23	Larceny	Life	Tin plate worker	Was Barker's servant during 1829. Pardoned 1839. Married Mary McGrogan 1832. Died after 1856.
Moxham	**James**	26	Uttering a forged note	14	Gunsmith and blacksmith	Married to Mary-Ann Rycroft. Freed 1833, died 1848, age 55.

Family[1] Name	Given Name	Age at court	Crime	Sentence	Occupation	Notes
*Murray	James	20	Stealing calico	7	Printer/sailor	Involved in affray in Dec 1827 when two Aborigines were shot and killed. Married Mary Ann Birchley, 1830. Died 1840, aged 55, Camperdown.
Neal	George	21	Burglary	Life	Seaman and navigator	Transported on the *Speke*, under guard by Lt Sleeman. Escaped by whaleboat on Oct 28, 1828, with Hassall, Richardson and Wales. Never seen again.
Oodeen		37	Desertion	Life	Drum major with the Malay Regiment	Employed as interpreter with the Macassans. Aka William O'Dean/O'Deen/Odeen. Mrs Oodeen and their five children also lived at FW.
Peacock	Joseph	28	Desertion	14	Soldier/ sawyer	Was the Second Overseer of Convicts. Apprehended for stealing corn. Freed in 1835.
Phillips	William	14	Stealing	Life	Tailer's apprentice.	Died either 1852 or 1856.
Potts	Thomas	26	House breaking	Life	Brick maker	Had been a 'tumbler' and entertained the Iwaidja with acrobatics they couldn't emulate (5 Feb Barker's journal). Died 1844, aged 46, Port Macquarie.

Family¹ Name	Given Name	Age at court	Crime	Sentence	Occupation	Notes
Richards	Joseph	21	Stealing boots and shoes	7	Shipwright	Confined to ship *Thompson* with Craggs and Sellers during preparations to abandon the fort in Aug 1827, as they were suspected of plotting to escape.
Richardson	William	21			Carpenter	Escaped by whaleboat on Oct 28, 1828, with Hassall, Neal and Wales. Never seen again.
Roberts	**William**	18	Stealing	14	Turner	Freed 1834.
Rushton	William	21	Burglary	Life	Brass founder	Pardoned 1840. Died 1849, aged 52, Parramatta.
Rycroft	**Mary Ann Moxham**	38		Life	Dress maker	Married to James Moxham. AKA Dianne Hughes. Died 1857, aged 69, Sydney.
Sellers	**Martin**	20	Stealing a watch	Life	Dyer	Confined to ship *Thompson* with Craggs and Richards during preparations to abandon the fort in Aug 1827, as they were suspected of plotting to escape. Returned to Sydney.
*Skelly	Patrick	32	Passing forged notes	14	Porter / carpenter	Transferred to King George's Sound in 1829. Ticket of Leave 1831 in Sydney.
Smith	James	30	Burglary (spoons).	Life	Hatter / blacksmith	Freed 1839.

Family[1] Name	Given Name	Age at court	Crime	Sentence	Occupation	Notes
Street	Joseph	37	House breaking	Life	Butcher	Tickets of Leave: 1836, 39 and 42. Campbelltown.
*Taylor	James			14		Speared by Iwaidja in the back 28 July 1827. Freed 1831.
Tobin	John	?	Stealing handkerchief	Life	Labourer	Stockman Freed and Pardoned 1838.
Trueman	Zacharia	19	Highway robbery	14	Blacksmith	Escaped for 3 days but returned for hunger.
Tuesman	George	21	Grand Larceny	7	Butcher	Left on the *Amity* as crew in March 1829, as freed January 1829. Died 1838, aged 37, Sydney.
Van Hammett	Joseph	25	Breaking house and stealing 2 pairs of stockings	Life	Sailor	A Belgian Sailor. Escaped to the bush when the settlement was abandoned. Assumed dead.
Wales	John	18	Burglary	Life	Shoemaker	Escaped by whaleboat on Oct 28, 1828, with Hassall, Richardson and Neal. Never seen again.

Sources of information: (Street, 2012) (Mulvaney, 1993) and others.
Names in **BOLD** identify Crown Prisoners who were transferred from Fort Dundas on Melville Island.
Those men marked * were invalided, died or were returned to Sydney during 1828.

Appendix 2
Letters and reports of note

Smyth to MacLeay, 18 July 1828

Captain Smyth was living at Emu Plains, near Sydney, when he was ordered by Colonial Secretary MacLeay to write an account of the fort in the time between his final official dispatch from Raffles Bay, and his departure on 24 April. Smyth sent MacLeay extracts from his diary and offered advice, from his experience, that would improve the chances of success in the settlement. Smyth recommended Port Essington as a better site for a settlement. He was not the only one to do so, and eventually the government was convinced. A new settlement, named Victoria after the new queen, would be formed there a decade later.

> *Sir, Emu Plains, 18th July 1828.*
>
> *I have the honor herewith to forward to you, for the information of His Excellency the Governor and in conformity with His Excellency's verbal instructions of the 7th instant, the daily occurrences at Raffles Bay Settlement from the period of my last despatches from thence, Dated 27th March, 1828, to that of my departure when I resigned the Command to Lieutenant Sleeman of the 39th Regiment.*
>
> *Wednesday, 16th April, At 11 A.M. Brig Philip Dundas and the Ship Marquis of Huntley arrived, the former with Dr. Davis and a Detachment of the 39th together with Stores for the Settlement; the Brig also brought 4 head of Cattle (1 Bull and 3 Cows),*

*11 Sheep and 94 in number of Turkeys, Ducks and Fowls; the
Marquis of Huntley is on her way from Batavia.*

*Thursday, 17th, Landed the Cattle and commenced landing of
the Stores. At 2 P.M., the Governor Phillip arrived with Captain
Hartley and Lieutenant Ovens, 57th Regiment, Doctor Sherwin,
Lieutenant Sleeman, 39th Regiment, and some Men for Melville
Island; also, four Crown Prisoners for this Settlement.*

*Friday, 18th, Hands employed as yesterday and got the whole of
the Stores on shore; at noon the Marquis of Huntley sailed, leaving
a perfectly new English built Whale boat with two sets of oars,
which I purchased for the use of the Settlement for £25 Sterling to
be paid to his agent in Sydney; the Garrison were much in need of
a boat, the old one being almost useless and no one to repair her,
the inconvenience of which I had seriously felt in not being able to
go any distance in search of the proahs.*

*At 2 P.M., 4 Canoes with Malays came in for water; six proahs
were in sight crossing the Bay from Bowen's Straits, where they
have been fishing, and report they have suffered by the hostility
of the Natives or as they call them Ourang Outang*; they proceed
to Port Essington to see Deing Riolo and get a supply of rice, etc.,
from him; I dismissed them with some bread and trifling presents.*

*Thursday, 24th April, having given over the Command of the
Settlement to Lieutenant Sleeman and explained to him ever
thing in my power relative to its future well-being, I embarked
the sick men selected by the Surgeons for Sydney, and at noon
went on board myself, weighed anchor and got out to sea that
afternoon. The foregoing are the principal occurrences of the day,
in addition to which I have only to make a few observations,
that by experience I am persuaded will tend to the advantage and
improvement of that Establishment.*

*1st. That a new Commissioned Officer and 10 or 12 Soldiers be
sent whenever supplies are forwarded, to enable the Commandant
to send a like number of sick or those who may have misbehaved
in return to Sydney.*

*2ndly. The withdrawing of the greater part of the Prisoners
which were first sent there and replacing them with others; their
constitutions, generally speaking, are much injured and with some
few exceptions very little assistance to advantage can be expected of*

---

* 'Forest men'.

them; a larger proportion of prisoners, a cooper, a Gardener and some few more mechanics, are much wanting. 3rdly. An Active man in the capacity of Constable with a pay so as to induce him to do his duty well, and subject to the power of the Commandant to be reduced and another put in his place.

Three or four Working Oxen (none of those already sent have reached Raffles Bay) with a small timber carriage, materials for boring for water.

I do not feel myself justified in forming an opinion as to the probability of realizing the views of His Majesty's Government in the formation of this Establishment as explained in His Excellency's Communication to me on that subject.

From the limited Communication with the Establishment, it can as yet be but little known; the Malays only have been there and for the sole purpose of fishing; until their arrival again on the coast next season, the result of my Communication with the Governor of Makassar and an English Merchant there cannot be known; that may probably throw some light on the subject. The disposition of the Malays appears to me harmless and inoffensive; their conduct while in Raffles Bay was strictly so.

Port Essington is decidedly their favorite rendezvous, and I regret exceedingly that the Settlement was not formed there; it possesses many important advantages, which Raffles Bay has not, and is, I have every reason to believe, inferior to none.

With regard to Climate there can be very little difference, but I conceive a better and more elevated ground could be selected at Port Essington and less contiguous to swamps than that of Raffles Bay. Having closed my proceedings to the period of my departure from Raffles Bay, I feel it a duty incumbent on me and in at necessity justice to myself to enclose to you, for the information of His Excellency, the Medical Certificate of my then impaired health and to assure you of my regret that it was not in my power to remain longer to witness the return of the Malays and to ascertain the result of my Communication with the Resident of Makassar with the probability of opening a more extended view of the eventual success of that Settlement.

I availed myself of the Confidence I felt in this worthy old man Deing Riolo to communicate the existence of the Settlement and the instructions I had received from His Excellency to the

Governor of Makassar and a Resident British Merchant there, Copies of which I beg to enclose as per Margin together with my last order when I resigned the Command to Lieutenant Sleeman of the 39th Regiment.

I have, &c, HY. SMYTH, Captn., 39th Regt. (Smyth, 18th July, 1828)

Captain Laws' report

Captain John M. Laws R.N., the commander of *HMS Satellite*, visited the northern settlements in September 1828, and again in July 1829. In 1828, he arrived at Raffles Bay direct from India, crossed to Fort Dundas, then sailed on to Sydney. He wrote a full account of both settlements, and they were among the first positive reports the government received. Unfortunately, by the time they arrived, it was too late to influence any decisions about the settlements' futures. Nevertheless, Laws' report on Raffles Bay provided important evidence which encouraged the next foray into settling the north, in Port Essington (Cameron, 2016).

... I found both the settlements at Raffles Bay and Melville Island amply supplied with fresh provisions, and perfectly healthy. At the former there were three in hospital, one soldier and two convicts; at the latter, they had not had a man on the sick list for two months before, or during our stay; and neither establishment had had an instance of death since the present officers arrived, which was in April last (1828).

At Raffles Bay there have been only three deaths since the formation of the settlement, the first of which was the surgeon. This circumstance left them without medical assistance for nearly seven months, during which period the other two died, an infant and a convict (disease not known).

At Melville Island I could not learn the number of deaths, there being no records on the island. At different times four or five had been killed by the natives, in consequence of coercive measures adopted towards them; since which they have quite estranged themselves from both settlements.

Since the formation of these settlements, they have been under the immediate military government of an officer of one of the regiments at Sydney, 'whose turn it was for detached duty', without reference to his habits, interest, or inclination; indeed, so far from the latter, that a Commandant at Melville Island told me that he hesitated whether he would not give up the army rather than go to that station; and since his arrival he has never been half a mile from the house he occupies; the consequence is, that what they have seen has been with jaundiced eyes, and their representations made accordingly, describing the climate to be such as to preclude the possibility of keeping the settlement, and the soil incapable of producing anything fit for the sustenance of man.

Now, looking at the number of deaths, and considering that every individual at both settlements are natives of Great Britain or Ireland; and that none of the officers, and not more than six of the men, had ever resided within the Tropics before, a tolerable estimate may be formed of the climate, which I do not hesitate to say is one of the best within the torrid zone,—indeed the difference we felt between it and India, was surprising. We had no instance of sickness during our stay in these seas, though I am convinced, had our people been as much exposed in wooding and watering in any part of either the East or West Indies, we should have had many cases of fever, if not of death. The principal disease appears to have been scurvy, the presence of which may be attributed to a want of the most ordinary precaution, owing to the inexperience of the individuals themselves, there being many indigenous roots and vegetables, among which are yams, arrowroot, and a kind of parsnip, together with a pea or calavance, and an abundance of the Palmyra cabbage, so invaluable to all the natives of Hindoostan. To obtain these, it is required to climb the tree, which they did not attempt, but procured a scanty supply by cutting it down to get a single cabbage; and none of the other vegetables have been used, except by two or three individuals, although the natives appear to almost live on the roasted yam.

The whole of the coast that we saw, from Cape Helvitius to Croker's Island, is well wooded; and, as far as the settlers have penetrated (about four miles), they have met with a variety of valuable timber—amongst which is the lignum-vitae, two kinds of teak, a native oak, a species of sandal-wood, and lance-wood, with several others well known and much used in India, from

145

their not being obnoxious to the worm or white ant, which none of the above are, according to the experience of the settlers, who found these insects wherever they have been, and the largest forest trees, of particular kinds, completely destroyed by them.

A singular characteristic of the country is, that, except just above high water mark, (where in most places it is overrun with mangroves,) there is no underwood; even in the thickest part of the forest the trees are a considerable distance apart, and between them the ground is covered with high grass, on which all the stock, whether brought from Sydney or Timor, appear to thrive very well.

During the dry season, by setting fire to the grass, a road is made sufficient to enable them, with the assistance of draft oxen, (which they have at Melville Island,) to choose their timber, and bring it in any quantities to the settlement.

I have landed, at the Colonial Dockyard here (Port Jackson), specimens of the timber at Melville Island, with the intention of sending it by the first transport to one of the dockyards in England for the inspection of the Commissioners of the Navy. I selected a common sized tree of the teak, oak, lignum-vitae, and blood-wood; the latter I was obliged to abandon, it being too large and heavy to carry on our decks through a boisterous latitude, I therefore only brought an arm of that tree, which, with the teak, would be very valuable at Calcutta or Madras, as well as in England.

With respect to the soil, everything that has been managed with the smallest knowledge of its properties, grows very well; but it would appear incredible, were I to attempt a description of the inconvenience they have experienced from not having any one familiar with the productions of a tropical climate.

On asking if they had attempted to grow rice, I was told that they had, but little of it came up; and on further inquiry, I found they had sown the clean rice, instead of the grain in its natural state of paddy,—this will give an idea of the clumsy way things have been done in these settlements.

At present all works are suspended under an impression that the two establishments are to be concentrated at Port Essington, which is certainly the most eligible port at present known for a principal settlement on the north coast of New Holland, being about four miles by land from Raffles Bay, and 170 by sea from Melville Island, and all three in the same degree of latitude.

I cannot help thinking it would be a great sacrifice to abandon those settlements, now the principal privations and difficulties, necessarily attending the formation of any new colony, are surmounted. It would be better to form another at Port Essington, it being the annual rendezvous of the Malays of Macassar and Arroe Islands, who come over with the end of the easterly monsoon, to collect and cure trepang for the China market; though last year finding there was an European settlement at Raffles Bay, three proas, with about thirty men in each, took their quarters up at the fort, and collected and cured what they could, so as to sail with the end of the monsoon. The natives are particularly hostile to the Malays, which made them very glad to have the protection of the fort.

I understand that one of the objects in forming these settlements was to open a trade with the Eastern Islands and China, which would be very easy from the great number of proas (ten or twelve per day having been seen from the fort) that annually visit the coast, from Macassar and the islands eastward, to collect and cure trepang for the Canton market; most of which bartered with the Dutch residents among the different islands, sent thence from Amboyna and Batavia, and from thence to China.

But, as a tropical climate must be uncongenial to the manual exertions of Europeans, I conceive it would be a much more efficient and less expensive plan to colonize New Holland principally from India.

Port Essington should be the penal settlement for the British possessions in the Indian seas; and every encouragement should be given to emigration from Calcutta and Madras, (in the miserable avenues of which hundreds are dying daily,) and at once a garrison should be formed, with two companies of the Ceylon regiment, with all their attendants; any of whom, by walking half a mile from the camp, would find plenty of the vegetables they had been accustomed to eat all their lives, which vegetables the English soldier (who thinks of no other resource than the commissariat) looked upon as poison.

I had an instance of this in my own servant, (a native of Trincomalee, and of the Gentoo cast,) who, in a quarter of an hour, collected vegetables to make a curry, and therefore to him a dinner.

At Timor as at Java, Malacca, and Penang, all the artisans are China men, who only require to know we have settlements on New Holland, to come over in great numbers, and their usefulness can only be truly estimated by those who have visited any of the above colonies … Reproduced from (Wilson, 1835).

Shipwrecks

Correspondence by Captain Nolbrow, of the *Mermaid*, to the *Colonial Times* giving an account of the wreck of the *Mermaid* and other shipwrecks in 1829:

> *… By the arrival of the ship Calista, Captain Hawkins, from Swan River, we regret to learn that the ship Swiftsure, Captain Johnstone, which sailed from this port the 3rd May, lastly from Sydney, bound for Batavia or the Mauritius; the ship Governor Ready, Captain Young, which also sailed from this port on the 2nd of April, for the Isle of France; and the brig Comet, Captain James Fraser, (which sailed from Hobart Town the 2nd February last, for Sydney), from Port Jackson for India; and the Government schooner Mermaid, of Sydney, Captain Nolbrow, formerly commander of the ship Jessie, have all been lost on the sunken rocks in Torres Straits. This information is derived from Captain Nolbrow, who was picked up by some vessel, and landed at Swan River, from whence he has arrived here in the Calista. We are glad to add, that no lives have been lost in any of these shipwrecks.*

> *Since writing the above, we have been favored with the following communication:*

> *SIR,--*

> *I request you will be pleased to insert, in your paper, for the information of the public and parties concerned, the loss and disasters of the following ships :*

> *Having sailed from Sydney on the 16th of May, in His Majesty's Colonial schooner Mermaid, bound to Port Raffles, with Government dispatches and provisions for King Georges Sound, under my command, and having proceeded the inner passage for Torres Straits, on the 13th June, at a quarter before six a.m. found the vessel strike on a sunken*

coral reef, with nine feet water on it, not laid down in Captain King's charts of the coast, in lat. 17° 7 S. long. 1 46° 10 E. with the following true bearings :--Fitzroy Island in a line with Cape Grafton, bearing N.W. 16 or 17 miles, the high peaked hill at Franklands Isles W. halt S. 9 or 10 miles, the coast of New Holland W. 16 or 17 miles ; the Mermaid was lost and abandoned the same evening, at 8 p.m.—the vessel bilged, and the water over the cabin deck.

The ship Governor Ready, Captain Young, in Torres Straits, going 8 knots, when she struck, and Captain Young and 1st mate on foretop-yard, at 3 p. m. on 18th May: the ships bows on the reef, and 7 fathoms water astern. No lives lost and reached Timor in their boats.

The brig Comet, which sailed in company with the brig Fairfield from Sydney parted in the night. The Comet lost on Boots reef—the crew picked up by the Fairfield, at Murrays Island.

The ship Swiftsure, Captain Johnstone, in the 13° 28 S near Cape Sidmouth, totally lost on the 4th of July. The crew and part of the cargo and stores saved by the brig Resource, and gone to the Isle of France.

The brig Resource having struck on Satellite Shoal, near Cape Flinders, got off—no material damage.

The ship Jupiter struck on the reef near Cairncross Island, received much damage, both pumps going, and gone to Java for repairs.

The schooner Admiral Gifford, of Sydney, Captain R. S. Walker, touched and unhung her rudder at Bloomfield River—not materially damaged.

The ship Marquis of Anglesea wrecked on the beach at Swan River and went ashore in a gale of wind.

The ship Parmelia struck on a coral—received much damage in steering in for Swan River. Hove down by His Majesty's ship Sulphur and sailed for the Isle of France.

The brig Governor Phillip arrived at Port Raffles about the 20th August, with the loss of two anchors, and about to sail for Copang and Swan River.

The brig Thompson taken up to convey Government stores to Swan River, sailed on the 25 August from Port Raffles. The brig Amity in company both arrived in Swan River on the 28 September. The brig Amity broke an anchor laying under Rottnest Island, and laying in Gages Roads, Swan River, with only one anchor on board, leaky, and expecting to go ashore if another gale set in.

His Majesty's Ship Satellite arrived at Port Raffles in the early part of August. The bark Reliance and the Thompson, in company having carried away her windlass in Torres Strait, saved by assistance from the Satellite, which was also nearly lost. The schooner Admiral Gifford arrived at Port Raffles—all well, and sailed for Copang for horses, for Swan River, and saw him at sea about 4th September, lat 15° S. 116°E, all well. Spoke the Kingsdown whaler, from London four months about the 6th September. 16° S.113 to 114° E, all well, which informed me of having spoke the Atwik, Captain Jeffreys, with a number of people on board for Swan River, amongst whom was Mr. Peel, who has a large grant of land.

The ship Calista, with all her anchors broken, lay in Gages Roads, and was in imminent danger of going on shore—fortunately saved by leaving it!

SAMUEL NOLBROW. Colonial Times Hobart, Tasmania. (Nolbrow, 30 October, 1829)

Appendix 3
Observations of the Iwaidja

The Iwaidja were among those tribes of the north coast of New Holland called 'Australians' by Matthew Flinders, in what was probably the first use of the term. They were described in detail by three of the diarists involved with the early settlement attempts: Dr Wilson, Captain Barker, and Major Campbell (in his address to the Royal Geographic Society in London). Campbell referenced a Captain Stoddart of the Royal Staff Corps (Campbell, 1834), but the latter's writing was only a summary of Dr Wilson's work. All the writers quoted below were class-conscious military career-men, rather than linguists, or anthropologists, and their observations are made through nineteenth-century English 'lenses', without any right of reply, and we need to remember, considering the language constraints, that they actually had very little verbal communication with the Iwaidja.

Campbell's Description of the Iwaidja:

... In personal appearance they bear some resemblance to the natives about Port Jackson: they are, however, better made and have more intelligent, and perhaps more savage countenances as they go entirely naked; their skin, particularly the breast and thighs, is ornamented, or disfigured with gashes; their hair is long, and generally straight, yet I observed some crisp. Some of them have a fillet of network about two or three inches wide bound

*tightly round the waist, with a similar ornament round the head
and the arms, and sometimes a necklace of network depending
some length down the back. Several of them have the front tooth
in the upper jaw knocked out in the manner described by Captain
Collins. They paint their face, and sometimes the entire body with
red earth: and those who are inclined to be dandies draw one
or two longitudinal lines of white across the forehead and three
similar on each cheek, while a few who appeared to be 'exquisites'
had another line drawn from the forehead to the tip of the nose.
The septum is invariably perforated; but it is on particular
occasions only that they introduce a bone or piece of wood through
it, and sometimes a feather. In this part of the coast the natives are
divided into three distinct classes-a circumstance quite unique ...
(Campbell, 1834).*

Iwaidja Social Divisions:

*... In this part of the coast, the natives are divided into three
distinct classes, who do not intermarry. The first and highest is
named Mandro-gillie, the second, Manbur-gē, and the third,
Mandro-willie.*

*The first class assumes a superiority over the others, which is
submitted to without reluctance; and those who believe in real
difference of blood amongst civilized nations, might find here some
apparent ground for such opinion, as the Mandro-gillies were
observed to be more polite, and unaffectedly easy in their manners,
than the others, who, it was supposed, were neither so shrewd nor
so refined: this, however, might be only imaginary.*

*Mariac (or Wellington as he was named by Captain Stirling),
the chief of the country round Raffles Bay and Port Essington, is
apparently about thirty-three years of age, nearly five feet eight
inches in height: he limps in his walk, but whether from a wound
received in foreign or domestic war, I did not learn. His features
are regular, and, while he is in a good humour, placid and
benign; but, on the least displeasure, which arose frequently from
slight causes, they gleamed with savage fury.*

*He has evidently much sway among his tribe; as even Miago,
although so much in favour with us, has been observed to fall
back, by a look and a word from his chief. From Miago's possessing*

a turn for fun and mimickry, and his unrivalled dexterity in throwing the spear, he had become a favourite in the camp, to the great annoyance of Wellington, who seemed to view him in the same light that Haman did Mordecai.

Wellington gave Captain Barker to understand, that presents to any of his people should only come through himself; and he occasionally exhibited so much ill-humour at deviations from this request, that Captain Barker thought it prudent to cut him for some time.

The natives generally go in parties of from six to twelve; Wellington, however, usually went at some distance apart, accompanied only by one. When the settlement was formed, his attendant was Iacama, a Manburge (called, by Captain Stirling, Waterloo).

Miago had then the honour of being his travelling companion, but lost the office, from the attention he received in the camp. He was succeeded by Olobo, a Mandrogillie, as timorous as a hare. When we left the settlement, Monanoo, the younger brother of the chief of Croker's Island, held that distinguished employment.

It is difficult to say whether they are accompanied in their excursions by their women, but it is probable that they are not. As far as we could learn, the natives never penetrate far into the interior, generally keeping along the shore, and occasionally cutting across any projecting point of land (Wilson, 1835).

The first and highest class are named 'Mandrogillies' the second; 'Manburghes' and the third 'Mandrowiles' The first class assume a superiority over the others, which is submitted to without reluctance; and those who believe in real difference of blood amongst civilized nations might find here some apparent ground for their belief: as the Mandrogillies were observed to be naturally more polite and unaffectedly easy in their manners than the others, who it was imagined were neither so shrewd nor so refined. This, however, might be only imaginary ... (Campbell, 1834).

Iwaidja Nature:

... Although it may appear rather paradoxical, yet I do not hesitate to say that these natives, far from being untameable savages as originally represented are in reality a mild and

153

merciful race of people. They appear to be fond of their wives and children—at least they talk of them-with much apparent affection. They have frequently interposed their good offices in preventing the children being chastised; I have seen them run between the mother and the child and beg the former to desist from her (as it appeared to them) unnatural conduct, in punishing her own offspring. They are like all other uncivilized people, very irascible, but easily pacified: they require to be managed like children. That they may be taught to distinguish conventional right from wrong was quite apparent; and many instances occurred that showed their aptitude in this respect. Iniago, after having become honest himself, once detected one of his companions endeavouring to secrete a spoon, while they were about to partake of some rice prepared for them; provoked by this ungrateful behaviour, he instantly took it from the delinquent and packed him off, without permitting him to have any share of the food. On first visiting the settlement, a native would invariably pilfer anything that came in his way that he could secrete; which, however, was always brought back by those who knew that such conduct was not countenanced by their civilized visiters [sic]: many instances of this kind occurred. They also soon learned to distinguish between a person whose word was to be depended on, and another of no veracity ... (Campbell, 1834).

Iwaidja Diet:

... Their food chiefly consists of fish, which they spear very dexterously. Catching turtle seems to be a favourite occupation with them, and they appear quite adept in that useful art. It is to point the spears, used for that purpose, that they estimate and covet iron so much. They also make use of shellfish, which it is probably the business of the women to collect. They do not eat the trepang (so desired by Chinese epicures), which is in great abundance all along the coast; but the various native esculent roots and fruits, together with cabbage-palms, afford an agreeable addition to their usual fare. [They are cleanly in their manners, and, in some respects, superior to the Europeans,—fulfilling the injunction of Moses in the twelfth and thirteenth verses of the twenty-third chapter of Deuteronomy.]

They are very fond of honey, which appears to be in abundance, as they were seldom seen in the settlement without a supply of that article; and when they went into the woods on purpose to procure it, they soon returned successful. Their mode of proceeding was, to watch the movements of the bees, (which requires a keen eye, and long practice,) and as soon as they saw them settle on a tree, they proceeded to cut it down, which they effected with their stone hatchets, much quicker than could be imagined. It was for this purpose that Waterloo ran away with the axe, 'after having seen and tried its use', judging, rightly, that it was preferable to his own ley-book (i.e. hatchet) … (Wilson, 1835).

Iwaidja Population:

… Respecting the number of the natives, there was no means of forming anything like a correct opinion; yet, judging from the rapidity with which they collected, when one of their countrymen was confined, it may be conjectured, that they are by no means thinly spread.

On the occasion alluded to, two natives, who had observed Luga taken into custody, left the settlement, and spread the tidings. In the evening, Wooloogary arrived, accompanied by fifty men at arms. From the time the two natives left, until Wooloogary's arrival, there was an interval of six hours; they had to walk two or three miles, and to cross and re-cross a strait two miles wide. It is difficult to know whether they would have acted hostilely, had their friend not been released; perhaps they only came to intercede in his behalf, and, according to the custom of civilized politicians, thought their request might be better attended to, by making a formidable appearance … (Wilson, 1835).

Iwaidja Weapons:

… The only warlike weapons that they used (as far as we could learn) were spears, of different forms and sizes; the largest are from nine to ten feet long: some are serrated and named burreburai; others are headed with a sharp stone and named imburbē. They use the throwing stick, named rogorook, which is exactly of the same form, and made in the same manner, as that in use among the natives about Port Jackson. Besides these, they have small

sharp-pointed spears, which they chiefly use in the spearing of fish (Wilson, 1835).

Their weapons are spears and clubs: the spears are about ten feet long, and lighter than those of Melville Island; and their war ones, named 'burreburai', instead of being barbed like a fishhook, as they are on Melville Island, are serrated like a saw. I should imagine from their weight that they are thrown from the hand without the lever which is used near Sydney and King George's Sound; but they are by no means so formidable as the Melville Island ones. Four of those of Port Essington fell on board a boat belonging to the brig Anne, but fortunately did no injury. They have others at Raffles Bay, called 'imburbé' headed with stone and also a small sharp-pointed spear for killing fish;-the clubs are rudely shaped, about four feet long and two inches in diameter (Campbell, 1834).

We could not learn whether they were in the habit of fighting with each other, or with neighbouring tribes; but spear wounds being by no means uncommon among them, it is probable that, in this respect, they also resemble their eastern Australian brethren. It is well known, however, that they wage continual war with the Malays, who, it was evident, both hated and feared them

It does not appear that the Marēge (the name given by the Malays to the natives) are altogether to blame, or, at least, they may plead in extenuation that, as the Mulwadie (as they call the Malays) come to their coasts without leave asked or obtained, and carry away the trepang, and, more particularly, the much-valued madjendie (i.e. Turtle), it is but fair that they should catch a canoe whenever they can; and that they are pretty successful in this way, appeared very evident to us,—all their canoes being of Malay construction ... (Wilson, 1835).

Iwaidja Praise:

... Although it may seem rather paradoxical, yet I do not hesitate to say, that the natives, far from being such untameable savages as originally represented, are, in reality, a mild and merciful race of people. They appeared to be fond of their wives and children; at least, they talked of them with much apparent affection. They have frequently interposed their good offices in preventing the

soldiers' children from being chastised: I have seen them run between the mother and child and beg the former to desist from her (as it appeared to them) unnatural conduct, in punishing her own offspring.

They are, like all uncivilized people, very irascible, but easily pacified; in short, they require to be managed just like children. They were easily taught to distinguish conventional right from wrong, and many instances occurred, which proved their aptitude in this respect ... (Wilson, 1835)

Iwaidja Honesty:

... Miago, after having become honest himself, once detected one of his companions endeavouring to secrete a spoon, while they were about to partake of some rice prepared for them;—provoked by this ungrateful behaviour, he instantly took it from the delinquent, and sent him away, without permitting him to have any share of the food.

On first visiting the settlement, a native would invariably pilfer anything that came in his way that he could secrete, but the article was always brought back by those who knew that such conduct was not tolerated by their civilized visitors.

They also soon learned to place confidence in a person whose word was to be depended on. Some of our people acted, perhaps, in rather a reprehensible manner, by promising the natives a mambrual (or some other present), merely to get rid of their importunities, without any intention of performing their promise, thinking the natives would forget the circumstance; but, in this supposition, they were completely deceived, being invariably and pertinaciously reminded of their promise, and the natives looked on them as not to be trusted in future;—on the contrary, they placed implicit reliance in those who, having given a promise, performed it punctually.

The chief objects of their desire were tomahawks, large nails, and iron hoops; but, in the progress of time, they took a fancy to various articles of dress. To obtain a shirt, was a great object with them; and they soon became so particular, that if a button were wanting in the collar or sleeves, they were not satisfied till the deficiency was remedied. A coloured handkerchief, which they used to roll neatly round the head, was also much prized.

After they became somewhat polished in their manner, if they saw anything that struck their fancy, they asked for it; if given them, they shewed no visible marks of thankfulness; and, if refused them with firmness, they laid it down quietly.

Sometime before we left the coast, they could be trusted implicitly, even with those articles they most highly prized ... (Wilson, 1835).

Iwaidja religion:

... Whether they have any idea of a Superior Being, or of a future state of existence, it was impossible for us to ascertain. It was easy enough to reciprocate communication, as far as regarded objects evident to the external senses; but, as may be imagined by those conversant on the subject, any attempt to talk of abstract principles must have proved altogether fruitless.

When it is called to mind that they were just beginning to lay aside suspicion, and to visit the settlement without fear, not long before it was abandoned, it will not seem strange that these particulars, relating to them, are so scanty and imperfect. A little longer intercourse would have enabled a person (inclined to observe their manners, and learn their language) to obtain more correct and extensive information respecting the various Aboriginal tribes on this part of the coast, who, to say the least of it, were treated so cavalierly, in the first instance, by the civilized intruders on their native land.

The Aborigines around Port Essington and its vicinity are the same in appearance with those of Melville Island; but their habits are somewhat distinct, and their weapons a little different They both go naked, are alike addicted to pilfering, and display similar characteristics of cunning; but I do not think the natives near Port Essington are so daring, in their enterprises. I never saw a Melville islander with an ornament beyond a feather in the hair, scarifying the body, and bedaubing the head, face, and every part of the skin with yellow, white, or red pigments. But on the Cobourg Peninsula the natives have a fillet of network bound round the waist and another round the head and arms, with sometimes a necklace; and they paint their bodies occasionally in the same manner as I have described in my account of the natives of Melville Island. Such of their canoes as I saw were hollowed from the trunks of trees, like those of the Malays, and were probably either left by these people or stolen from them, for I do not think they have any means of hollowing them out themselves … (Campbell, 1834).

Iwaidja Gravesite:

… I remarked one native burial-place at Port Essington: it was near Native Companion Plain. The grave was very simple and placed under a widely spreading tree. The space occupied was six feet long by three wides, over which was formed an open framework of twigs, the ends being inserted in the ground on each side. Upon the grave lay a skull, evidently of an Aborigine, with a thigh or arm bone; the skull was coloured red, as if with some dye, and the teeth appeared as if they had been burnt … (Campbell, 1834).

Some Iwaidja words:

The nineteenth century was a time of great interest in native peoples across the world. Collectors of artefacts could make a good living collecting everything from beads and spears, to the bones of the dead, and collections of word lists added to their mystique. Dr Wilson was keen to learn some Iwaidja language, and he prepared a list of vocabulary for his book, although he admitted he found it difficult to hear the words clearly:

… The dialect of the natives of Raffles Bay is by no means inharmonious, but it was extremely difficult to obtain the true sound of their words, as it frequently happened, that the words (the correct sound of which not being caught at first) were repeated by us as near as we could guess, when they, either through indifference or complaisance, adopted our mode of pronunciation; and it required some pains, on our part, to obviate the effects of their apathy or inconvenient politeness … (Wilson, 1835).

Others were interested in language as well, as this letter from an unknown writer[*] at Fort Wellington, published in *The Sydney Gazette*

[*] The author was not Wilson or Barker because the spelling is very different to

and New South Wales Advertiser on 25 June 1829, shows:

Port Raffles.

The diversity of the aboriginal language is most remarkable, and we have an additional instance of it in a small vocabulary lately handed to us, by a gentleman who had received it from an intelligent friend at Port Raffles*. It has been compared with the dialect of the tribes in our own vicinity, to which it scarcely bears the most distant resemblance, except as to the general character of its orthoepy†. To the list we subjoin a few remarks by the compiler.

The head is called ... Weeya

The hair ... Warree

The nose ... Innee

The mouth ... Lowell

The eye ... Indella

The hand ... Murrawee

The teeth ... Erayen

A foot ... Eelood

A shoe ... Yallagoodyeny

Chin or beard ... Lammormow

Water ... Oboit

Fire ... Juno

Boat or ship ... Oboy

An iron nail ... Wallemooroo

Iron ... Wilmore

Wood ... Yajack or araback

A stone ... Arickbah

Hatchet ... Leeboy

Basket (small) ... Moolack

Ditto (large) ... Mulberragin

Musket ... Mulberragin

The red apple ... Wellawella

A large lizard ... Monologoro

Turtle ... Maghindu or Manbegee

Bread ... Carga

Fish ... Armidhee

Bag ... Annodonye

Woman ... Yalcookie

Brother ... Naddyaman

Asleep ... Googoogoo

By and bye ... Googoo

Stone-headed spear ... Imbocubee

Serrated ditto ... Booribooray

Throwing stick ... Rogro

The sun ... Mourhay

The moon ... Alahay

Yes ... Ee

No ... No

Cockatoo ... Marbite

Musquitoe ... Minming

Fly ... Mourt.

Titles of the Chiefs. A chief or gentleman is called Mandiaragelly. His Prime Minister is called Malbulgy. Next to him is called Mandioroly or Mandiorowillie. Capt. Smyth titled the Chief

---

vocabulary lists published in their journals.

* Both Captain Barker and Dr Wilson made wordlists of Iwaidja language, sometimes with marked spelling differences (see Mulvaney 1992). Father Angelo Confalonieri wrote a phrase book, ten years later, which included many Iwaidja 'Garig' words (many of which are now extinct). None of these men were trained linguists, but their contributions are valuable. For more on Iwaidja language see (Birch, 2014)

† 'Orthoepy' = correct pronunciation of words.

*"Wellington," and his Malbulgy "Waterloo," which names they
still retain.*

*We have one of them frequently in the camp (Mago), who is
an intelligent fellow, and is an excellent mimic. They do not
distinguish the difference, with any degree of nicety, between
meum and tuum, but I do not look on them as professed thieves.
Hatchets and handkerchiefs are the most desirable presents ; they
give everything they get to the women; we have not seen any of
them as yet'* (Letters, Sydney Gazette *25 June 1829).*

Bibliography

Allen, J., 1973. *The Archaeology of Nineteenth-Century British Imperialism: An Australian Case Study.* World Archaeology 5: pp. 44–60.

Allen, J., 2008. *Port Essington: The Historical Archeology of a North Australian Nineteenth-Century Military Outpost.* Sydney: Australian Society for Historical Archeology, Sydney University Press.

Almanac, 1830. *Australian Almanac for the Year of Our Lord 1831.* [Online] Available at: https://books.google.com.au/books?id=9spbAAAAQAAJ&pg [Accessed 6 November 2019].

Annabel, R., Betteridge, M., Marks, C. & Morris, C., 2003. *Port Macquarie Former Government House Ruins Conservation Management Plan.* 1 ed. Port Macquarie: NSW Heritage Office.

Australian, The, 29 June 1927. *Guards.* Sydney: The Australian.

Bach, J., 1958. *Melville Island and Raffles Bay, 1824–9: An Unsuccessful Settlement,.* Journal of the Royal Historical Society of Australia, Vol. 44(4), pp. 233–7.

Barker, Collett, 12 August 1829. *Barker to Naval Commander in Chief, India.* Historical Records of Australia, Series III, Vol. VI.

——, 1829. *Journal of Captain Collet Barker,* (in Mulvaney and Green, 1992). Melbourne: The Miegunyah Press.

——, 21 Sept 1828. *Barker to MacLeay.* Historical Records of Australia, Series III, Vol. VI.

——, 22 August 1829. *Barker to MacLeay.* Historical Records of Australia, Series III, Vol. VI.

——, 23 October 1829. *Barker to MacLeay.* Historical Records of Australia, Series III, Vol. VI.

——, 26 February 1829. *Barker to MacLeay.* Historical Records of Australia, Series III, Vol. VI.

——, 7 August 1829. *Charter of Brig Thomson (sic).* Historical Records of Australia, Series III, Vol. VI, pp. 833–4.

Bathurst, E. H., 1826. *Letter: Bathurst to Governor Ralph Darling,*. Historical Records of Australia, Series I, Vol. XII, p. 224.

Bauer, F., 1964. *Part 2: The Katherine–Darwin Region.* Historical Geography of White Settlement in Part of Northern Australia. Canberra: CSIRO.

BDA, 2019. *Biographical Data Base of Australia: 39th Regiment of Foot.* [Online] Available at: https://www.bda-online.org.au/files/MR10_Military.pdf [Accessed 12 November 2019].

BDA, 2019. *Biographical Database of Australia: 39th Regiment of Foot.* [Online] Available at: https://www.bda-online.org.au/files/MR10_Military.pdf [Accessed 6 November 2019].

Birch, B., 2014. *Nagoyo. The Life of Don Angelo Confalonieri Among the Aborigines of Australia 1846–1848.* The Australasian Catholic Record, Vol. 91, No. 1, Jan 2014: pp. 117–9.

Bown, R., 2003. *Scurvy: How a Surgeon, a Mariner and a Gentleman Solved the Greatest Medical Mystery in the Age of Sail:* Viking.

Brookshaw, T., 2013. *The Long Expedition to Fort Dundas, Melville Island, Northern Australia.* Northern Territory Historical Studies, Issue 24, 2013, pp. 74–89.

Cameron, J., 2016. *Stakes in a Ring Fence.* Northern Territory Historical Studies: A Journal of History, Heritage and Archeology, 1(27), pp. 1–25.

Campbell, J., 1834. *Geographical Memoir of Melville Island and Port Essington, on the Cobourg Peninsula.* London: The Journal of the Royal Geographical Society of London, Vol. 4 (1834), pp. 129–81.

Cannon, R., 1853. *Historical Record of the Thirty-Ninth, or Dorsetshire Regiment of Foot.* London.

Clark, M. A., 2013. *Maccassan History and Heritage: Journeys, Encounters and Influences.* Canberra: ANU Press.

Collins, D., 1798. *An Account of the English Colony in New South Wales with Remarks on the Dispositions, Customs, Manners, etc. of the Native Inhabitants of that Country to Which Are Added, Some Particulars of New Zealand.* http://gutenberg.net.au/:.

Committee, 4 August 1835. *Report of the Select Committee on Colonial Military Expenditure Together with Minutes of Evidence and an Appendix and Index.* London: House of Commons.

Connor, J., 2002. *The Australian Frontier Wars, 1788–1851.* University of New South Wales Press.

d'Urville, J. S. C. D., 1839. *An Account in Two Volumes of Two Voyages to the South Seas by Captain Jules S-C Dumont D'Urville of the French Navy (Vol 2) to the Straits of Magellan, Chile, Oceania, South-East Asia, Australia, Antarctica, New Zealand and Torres Strait, 1837–1840.* In 'The Visit of the Astrolabe and the Zéllée' by

MacKight, C.C., 1969, 'The Farthest Coast': MUP.

——, 1839. *The Visit of the Astralobe and the Zélée.* In MacKight, C.C., 1969 'The Farthest Coast': MUP.

Darling, R., 25 February 1828. *Darling to Huskisson.* CO 201/191: In Graham, G. Great Britain in the Indian Ocean, Clarendon Press, 1967.

Davis, D. R., 1829. *Annual Medical Report from June 21st, 1828, to June 20th, 1829.* In Wilson, T.B., 1835, A Narrative of a Voyage Round the World.

Duncan, D., 1827. *Diary of Dr Duncan,* Chapter IX: Quoted in Wilson, T.B., 1835, A Narrative of a Voyage Round the World.

Earl, G. W., 1846. *Enterprise in Tropical Australia.* British Library: Historical print edition. London: Madden and Malcolm.

Flinders, M., 1803. *The Voyage of H.M.S. Investigator.* In MacKinght, C.C., 1969, 'The Farthest Coast', p. 61: MUP.

——, 1814. *A Voyage to Terra Australis Vol 2.* Pall Mall: Nicol, G. and W.

Foelsche, P., 1886. *The Australian Race.* In Curr, Edward Micklethwaite (ed.). *The Australian race: its origin, languages, customs, place of landing in Australia and the routes by which it spread itself over the continent.* [Online]
Available at: https://ia802205.us.archive.org/3/items/australianracei01currgoog/australianracei01currgoog.pdf
[Accessed 17: Foelsche, Paul (1886). 'Raffles Bay: The Unalla Tribe'. Nov 2019].

Frederickson, C. & DeLaRue, C., 2013. *Settlement of Solitude: an Assessment of the Site of Fort Wellington, Raffles Bay.* in Northern Territory Historical Studies: 2013, p. 4.

Gazette, 10 March 1825. *Extracts from the Journal of 'An Officer of the Expedition',* Sydney Gazette and New South Wales Advertiser, Volume http://trove.nla.gov.au.

——, 18 June 1828. *Port Raffles.* Sydney Gazette and New South Wales Advertiser, p. 2.

Graham, G., 1967. *Great Britain in the Indian Ocean: A Study of Maritime Enterprise 1810–1850.* Oxford: Clarendon Press.

Gregory, R., 1996. *Fort Wellington Raffles Bay Heritage Evaluation.* Darwin: NTG.

Griffiths, R., February 1836. *The Monthly Review: January to April Inclusive.* London Vol. 139.

Harris, J., 1985. *Contact Languages at the Northern Territory British Military Settlements 1824-29.* [Online]
Available at: http://press-files.anu.edu.au/downloads/press/p71761/pdf/article083.pdf [Accessed 1 November 2019].

Hartley, H., 1829. *Hartley to MacLeay.* Historical Records of Australia, Series III, Vol. V, pp. 729–32.

——, 1828. *Letter: Hartley to Alexander Macleay, Colonial Secretary.* Historical Records of Australia, Series III, Vol. V, 8 September, pp. 760–3.

Hartwig, M., 2007. *Respect and understanding versus arrogance: A study of how the approach of nineteenth-century British military commander in the Northern Territory, Collet Barker, offers a positive path towards intercultural interaction in Australia.* https://espace.cdu.edu.au/eserv/cdu:60819/Thesis_CDU_60819_Hartwig_M.pdf.

Hill, E., 1951. *The Territory.* Angus and Robertson.

Hordern, M., 1989. *Mariners are Warned: John Lort Stokes and HMS Beagle in Australia 1837–1843.* 2002 ed. Melbourne: MUP.

HRA, 1827c. *Inquiry re Capture of Native Child and Encounter with Natives.* Fol. 683 CO201/193. Historical Records of Australia.

HSNT, 1971. *An Account of the Expedition to Fort Wellington, Raffles Bay, N.T. From 20th August to 2nd September 1966.* Darwin: Historical Society of the Northern Territory Inc.

Hunter, C., 2015. *The 1827 Newcastle Notebook and Letters of Lieutenant William S Coke H.M. 39th Regiment.* https://hunterlivinghistories.com/wp-content/uploads/2015/11/coke-1827.pdf ed. Ed. Cynthia Hunter: Hunter House Publications.

Innes, B., 2019. *Captain of Solitude: the Collett Barker Story.* ISBN 9781642555608 ed. Google Books.

James, B., 1989. *No Man's Land: Women of the Northern Territory.* Collins.

King, P. P., 1827. *Narrative of a survey of the intertropical and westeren coasts of Australia performed between the years 1818 and 1822.* Online ed. London: https://play.google.com/books.

——, 1827. *Narrative of the Survey of the Coasts of Australia Performed between the years 1818 and 1822.* http://gutenberg.net.au/ebooks/e00027.html ed. London: John Murray.

Leichhardt, D. I., 1847. *Journal of an Overland Expedition in Australia 1844–5.* Les Hiddon Series, 2000 Adelaide: Corkwood Press.

MacKnight, C., 1969. *The Farthest Coast: A Selection of Writings Relating to the History of the Northern Coast of Australia.* Edited: Melbourne University Press.

——, 2017. *The Voyage to Marege: Macassan Trepangers in Northern Australia.* 2nd ed. Melbourne: Melbourne University Press.

MacLeay, A., 14 August 1828. *MacLeay to Barker.* Historical Records of Australia, Series III, Vol. VI, p. 813.

May, S. K., Taçon, P. S., Wesley, D. & Pearso, M., 2013. *Painted Ships on a Painted Arnhem land Landscape.* The Great Circle, Published by: Australian Association for Maritime History, Vol. 35, No. 2, (Special Issue: Maritime Rock Art, 2013), pp. 83–102.

Monitor, 4 October, 1827. *The Monitor:* Sydney.

Moodie, G., 2019. *At World's End.* [Online]
Available at: https://www.abc.net.au/news/2019-12-03/port-essington-worlds-end-failed-british-colonial-settlement. [Accessed 5 December 2019].

Mulvaney, D., 1993. *The Search for Collet Barker of Raffles Bay.* Occasional Papers No. 44, State Library of the Northern Territory.

Mulvaney, D. & Green, N., 1992. *Commandant of Solitude.* (Including the Journal of Captain Barker), The Miegunah Press.

Nolbrow, S., 30 October, 1829. *Perils of the Sea.* The Colonial Times Hobart, p. 3.

Papers, 4 August 1835. *Report from the Select Committee on Military Spending.* [Online]
Available at: https://books.google.com.au/books Captain+Smyth
[Accessed 6 November 2019].

Powell, A., 2016. *World's End: British Military Outposts in the 'Ring Fence' Around Australia 1824–1849.* Melbourne: Australian Scholarly.

Pugh, D., 2017. *Fort Dundas, The British in North Australia 1824–29.* Darwin: www.derekpugh.com.au.

——, 2018. *Escape Cliffs: The First Northern Territory Expedition 1864–66.* Darwin: www.derekpugh.com.au.

Reid, B., 2011. *A Colonial Enigma Resolved: The Rediscovery of Fort Wellington, Cobourg Peninsula.* Darwin: Historical Society of the Northern Territory.

Rogers, F., 1982. *Port Macquarie, a History to 1850.* Hastings District Historical Society: Child and Henry Publishing.

Rootsweb, 2019. *Members of the 39th regiment.* [Online]
Available at: http://freepages.rootsweb.com/~garter1/history/surnames39th.htm
[Accessed 6 November 2019].

SBS, 2019. *Mermaid Wreck Found in Reef Waters.* [Online]
Available at: https://www.sbs.com.au/news/mermaid-wreck-found-in-reef-waters
[Accessed 20 November 2019].

Sleeman, G., 22 April 1828. *Lieutenant Sleeman To Colonial Secretary Macleay. 1828, 22 April.* (Despatches No. 1–3). Historical Records of Australia, Vol. VI, Despatch No. 1–3.

Smyth, C. H., August 1827. *Smyth to Macleay: Dispatch No. 3.* Historical Records of Australia, Vol. VI, : Despatch No. 3, p. 770.

——, 10 June 1827. *Smyth to MacLeay, Dispatch No. 1.* Historical Records of Australia, Vol. VI.

——, 12 February 1828. *Smyth to Macleay.* Historical Records of Australia, Ser. III, Vol. VI, p. 781.

——, 1827 diary. *Diary of Henry Smyth.* Extracts printed in Wilson, T.B., 1835, A Narrative of a Voyage Round the World.

——, 1827a. *Smyth to Macleay.* Historical Records of Australia, Ser. III, Vol. VI, 19 June.

——, 1827b. *Smyth to Governor Darling.* Historical Records of Australia, Ser. III, Vol. VI, pp. 818–9.

——, 1828c. *Medical Certificate: Enclosure No 1.* In Smyth to MacLeay 18 July. Historical Records of Australia, Ser. III, Vol. VI, p. 805.

——, 18th July, 1828. *Smyth to MacLeay, Emu Plains, NSW.* Historical Records of Australia, Ser. III, Vol. VI.

——, 9 July 1827. *Smyth to MacLeay Dispatch No. 2.* Historical Records of Australia, Ser. III, Vol. VI.

——, Dispatch #3, 17 July 1827. *Smyth to MacLeay.* Historical Records of Australia, Ser. III, Vol. VI, Fort Wellington.

——, Feb 1828. *Smyth to MacLeay.* in Historical Records of Australia, pp. 781–9.

Statham-Drew, P., 2003. *James Stirling: Admiral and Founding Governor of Western Australia.* University of Western Australia Press.

Steuart, G., 19 Sept 1834. *Supplement to The London Gazette,* Vol. No. 19193.

Stirling, J., 22 July 1827. *Stirling to Smyth.* Historical Records of Australia, Ser. III, Vol. V, p. 816, HMS Success.

——, 1827. *Despatch No. 100 from General Darling Governor of NSW to Lord Bathurst, Public Records Office, Kew. CO 201/193 #88355, p. 56,* Volume 'Settlement of Solitude', Quoted in Frederickson and De la Rue, p. 4.

——, 8 June 1828. *Stirling to Admiralty.* Historical Records of Australia, Ser. III, Vol. III, p. 815.

Street, E., 2012. *Distant Settlements: Convicts in Remote Australia.* Darwin: Historical Society of the Northern Territory.

Sturt, C., 1835. *Sturt's Two Expeditions into the Interior of South Australia.* In Wilson, T.B., 1835, A Narrative of a Voyage Round the World, Vol. II, p. 239.

Taçon, P. S. & May, S. K., 2013. *Ship Shape: An Exploration of Maritime-Related Depictions in Indigenous Rock Art and Material Cultureship Shape: An Exploration of Maritime-Related Depictions in Indigenous Rock Art and Material Culture.* Australian Association for Maritime History, The Great Circle, Vol. 35, No. 2, (Special Issue: Maritime Rock Art, 2013), pp. 7–15.

Taçon, P. S. et al., 2010. *A Minimum Age for Early Depictions of Southeast Asian Praus: In the Rock Art of Arnhem Land, Northern Territory.* Australian Archaeology, No. 71 (Taylor & Francis, Ltd), pp. 1–10.

Thomas, R., 1828. *Modern Practice of Physic.* [Online]
Available at: https://archive.org/details/modernpracticep01thomgoog/page/n784
[Accessed 6 November 2019].

Turner, C., 25 May 1825. *Letter: Assistant Surgeon Turner to Major Ovens.* Historical
Records of Australia, Volume Series III, Vol VI, p. 650.

Uptin, C., 1957. *The History of Port Macquarie.* 1983 revised ed. Port Macquarie: Hastings
District Historical Society.

White, O. G. W., 1955. *The Dorset Regiment in Australia.* Australian Army Journal, August
1955, (No 75), pp. 5–12.

Wilson, T. B., 1835. *Narrative of a Voyage Round the World.* This edition published by
Franklin Classics ed. London: Originally published by Sherwood, Gilbert and Piper.

Index

Further reading
History books by Derek Pugh, OAM

ESCAPE CLIFFS
The First Northern Territory Expedition 1864–66

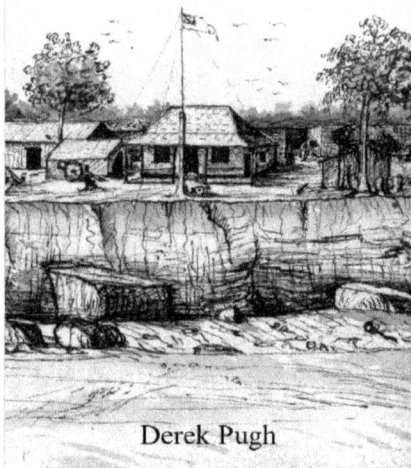

ESCAPE CLIFFS

The First Northern Territory
Expedition 1864-66

Derek Pugh

This is the true story of South Australia's first attempt at colonising their Northern Territory. It is a story of greed, courage, exploration, murder, wasted efforts, life and death struggles, insubordination, incredible seamanship, and extraordinary bushmanship, amid government bungling and Aboriginal resistance.

The South Australians wanted their state to be the *premier* state of Australia. The new settlement was expected to open up a trading route across the country, to Asia and beyond, and exploit the agricultural and mining opportunities of the interior. It was to be at no cost to the state, as the land was sold, unseen and unsurveyed, to investors in Adelaide and London, prior to the First Northern Territory Expedition even setting out.

The investors were already calculating their returns, but then, as the saying goes, the fight really started …

A fantastic read: insightful, cohesive, sequential, and well-paced. Loved it. Plenty of photos and maps to set the scene, with the addition of well researched complementary, first-hand accounts and primary records. Pugh has captured the essence of the time, place and characters: their personalities, hardships, successes and celebrations. I wanted to read it to find out what was going to happen next. Pugh's writing style is 'alive' and easy to read. Jill Finch

www.derekpugh.com.au

The British in North Australia 1824–29
FORT DUNDAS

Fort Dundas was the first outpost of Europeans in Australia's north. It was a British fortification manned by soldiers, marines and convicts, and built by them on remote Melville Island, in 1824. The fort struggled on until February 1829, when it was abandoned and left to the termites.

The fort's purpose was twofold. First, it was a physical demonstration of Britain's claim to the New Holland continent, as far as longitude 129°E, and thus excluded the Dutch and the French from starting similar colonies on the north coast. It was the first of a series of fortified locations around the coast. Second, it would be the start of a British trading post that would become a second Singapore, and compete with Batavia.

The settlement was named in a ceremony on 21 October 1824, but it was not a success. From its short existence come tales of great privation, survival, greed, piracy, slavery, murder, kidnapping, scurvy, and battles with the Indigenous inhabitants of the islands, the Tiwi.

It was also the site of the first European wedding and the birth of the first European children in northern Australia.

None of the three military commandants who managed the outpost wanted to be there and all were gratefully relieved after their posting. They left behind thirty-four dead—victims of disease, poor diet and Tiwi spears. Others died when the crews of the fort's supply ships were slaughtered and beheaded by Malay pirates on islands to the north. Two cabin boys from one of them, the *Stedcombe*, were enslaved by the pirates.

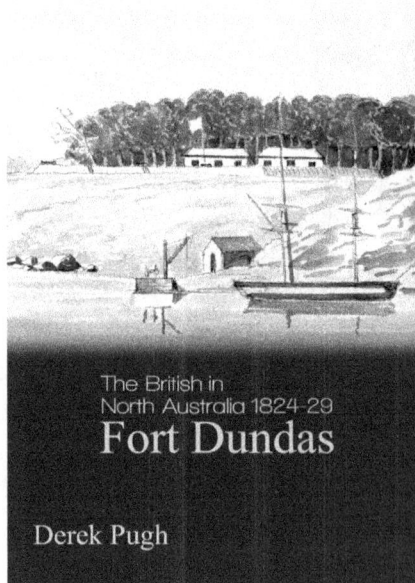

The story of what happened at Fort Dundas and why it was abandoned has been largely untold. Nevertheless, it is one of the most engaging stories of nineteenth-century Australia, presented here in Derek Pugh's usual captivating style.

The British in North Australia 1824–29
Fort Dundas

Derek Pugh

www.derekpugh.com.au

DARWIN 1869
The Second Northern Territory Expedition

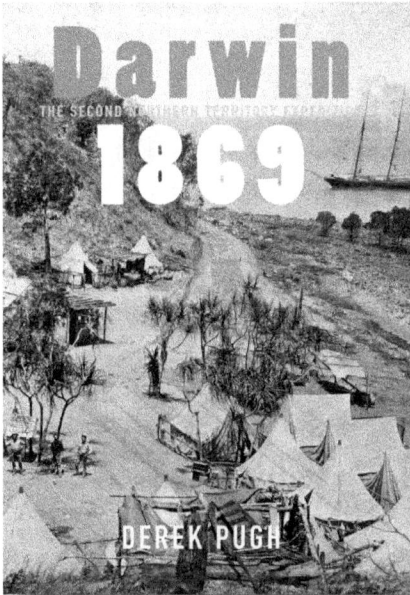

The Northern Territory had its beginnings under the governance of South Australia. Land was sold to investors, unseen and unsurveyed and in an unknown location. The sales raised the funds needed and The First Northern Territory Expedition was sent north to make it a reality, but it failed miserably, and the government faced huge losses with insufficient reserves to refund its investors.

To mitigate the loss, a new venture was envisaged—the Second Northern Territory Expedition, and there was only one man thought capable of ensuring a successful survey of the north: The Surveyor General, George Woodroffe Goyder.

Goyder was an extraordinary man, full of frenetic energy and with a phenomenal work ethic. The survey took him, and his expert teams of surveyors and bushmen, only eight months. It resulted in the laying out of the city of Palmerston (now called Darwin), three rural towns and hundreds of rural blocks, spreading over almost 270,000 hectares, all pegged out in the bush and Larrakia and Wulna lands—without permission or compensation—and conflict with the Aborigines was an ever-present danger. Two men were speared, one of them fatally.

Darwin grew from these somewhat humble but tumultuous beginnings. It was the only pre-Federation Australian capital established late enough to be photographed from its first settlement; and it is a survivor of challenges and privations unheard of in more temperate climes.

Darwin's story is written on its maps. Street names such as Knuckey, McLachlan, Daly, Wood, Bennett, Harvey and Smith Street recall the surveyors and their teams. Suburbs such as Millner, Larrakiyah, Bellamack and Stuart Park also remind us of the city's earliest days. It is the story of how the courage and diligence of a few led to the founding of the unique city of Darwin.

www.derekpugh.com.au

DARWIN: Origin of a City

A crocodile pulls a sleeping man into the river by one leg. Another breaks the neck of a swimming policeman. An out-of-luck miner drowns himself in the town's well.

Once called Palmerston, the City of Darwin was settled in the 1870s. It was a pioneer's paradise; sometimes as exciting as it was dull; full of potential but, too often, dangerous. Not everyone survived.

The first settlers arrived in January 1870, to find very little other than surveyed blocks of bushland sold to distant investors. It was a colony made from scratch, with little tangible reason for its existence until the Overland Telegraph Line came through from London and joined Australia to the rest of the world. Then gold was discovered, and hopeful miners rushed north from all over the country. Most went home disappointed; but only if they survived the privations of the bush and the distraction of the pubs. Then the government brought in Chinese 'Coolie' workers—and they kept coming, gold dust shining in their eyes, until, by the end of the decade, there were ten times as many Chinese as European settlers, and

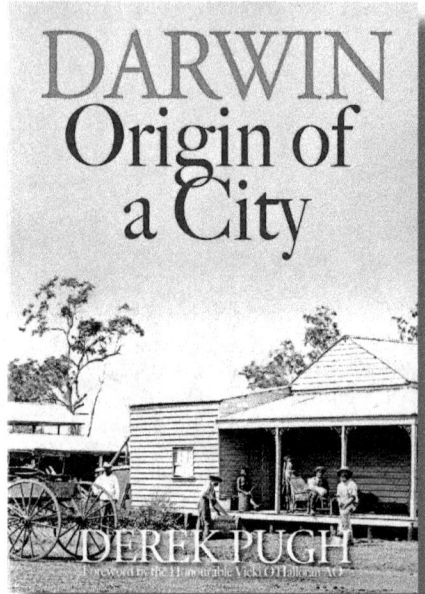

Chinatown was the most vibrant part of the settlement.

Known as Palmerston until it was renamed in 1911, Pugh brings the early colony to life once again, through this delightful and colourful account of Darwin's fascinating, unique early history, and the extraordinary characters who pioneered the settlement of the north.

Short listed
Chief Minister's Northern Territory History Book Award, 2020

www.derekpugh.com.au

Turn Left at the Devil Tree

A memoir and history set in the remotest parts of Arnhem Land. Derek Pugh, an ex-Kakadu ranger, teacher, naturalist, bushman, and historian, worked in several homelands schools and joined a lifestyle as old as time among the Indigenous peoples of central Arnhem Land.

His memoir is by turns reflective, tragic and hilarious and describes a life, in remote Aboriginal Australia, which gave him an insight into a traditional culture which has been witnessed by few outsiders.

Life there was 'frustrating at times, but always a challenge and Derek has recorded his experiences beautifully in this delightful book'. Ted Egan AO

Spending more than twenty years among the people and wildlife of the Top End of the Northern Territory, Derek Pugh revelled in the lifestyle and freedom of the bush. Told with respect and candour

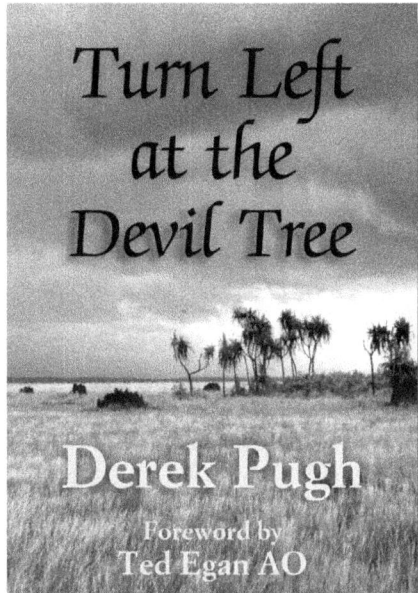

Turn Left at the Devil Tree is Pugh's 'slice of history'.

www.derekpugh.com.au

www.ingramcontent.com/pod-product-compliance
Lightning Source LLC
Chambersburg PA
CBHW071955090426
42740CB00011B/1956